Whenever I need a good belly laugh, a dose of truth, and a dash of inspiration, I turn to Kerri Pomarolli. With this book, Kerri hands us a mirror and a makeup wipe and reminds us we don't have to cover up the real us.

Tricia Goyer, bestselling author of *The Grumble-Free Year*

Through her comedy, honesty, wit, and vulnerability, Kerri reminds us that God isn't holding a competition for the perfect woman. Kerri leads her readers to discover their own uniqueness in God's image and guides us on an ultra-fun quest of accepting ourselves as God's beautiful creation.

Dr. Susie Shellenberger, bestselling author and speaker

There are only a few authors who can put Patrick Swayze, King David, and Clark Gable in the same paragraph. Kerri Pomarolli is one of them! Kerri writes with warmth, candor, and of course her signature humor.

Arlene Pellicane, speaker and author of *31 Days to Becoming a Happy Mom*

We all want to be that all put-together Proverbs 31 Woman, but life is imperfect. So what do we do on those less-than-perfect days? Read and get encouragement, a laugh, and a lift-up from Kerri and this Proverbs 32 treatise of hope, humor, and help!

Pam Farrel, author of *Men Are Like Waffles, Women Are Like Spaghetti*

Kerri always makes me laugh and feel accepted in my imperfection, and who isn't in need of that? I love this woman and her wild and truthful storytelling.

Lisa Whittle, author and podcast host of *Jesus Over Everything*

You know those times when you are pretty sure you have got this adulting thing all wrong, and you are sure everyone else read a handbook you were never given? Kerri encourages us to embrace the hot mess in all of us. Her words will not only make you laugh but will remind you that you are not alone.

Melissa d'Arabian, author of *Tasting Grace*

Kerri's "Type AAA" personality hilariously shines through these pages as she allows us to peer through the smudged window of her chaotic life where faith in God, raw honesty, and vats of Nutella are her weapons of mass destruction against perfectionism. Through raucous anecdotes and totally doable practical applications, she knocks the stuffing out of self-deprecating fault-finding and sets us free to serve the Lord—just as we are.

T. Faye Griffin, author of *Morning Manna*

This book had me laughing out loud and also wiping away tears as I related with the struggle to measure up to Proverbs 31 standards. Kerri Pomarolli shares her real-life stories with humor and a hunger to follow Jesus, seeking imperfect progress rather than faking perfection.

Melissa Spoelstra, speaker and Bible teacher

If comedy doesn't come from a place of truth, the funny exits stage right. And it's Kerri's unabashed honesty that makes her book so wonderful! When you find yourself in this book, you'll be encouraged that you're not alone in this chaotic but glorious journey.

Dan Rupple, CEO, Mastermedia International

CONFESSIONS OF A
PROVERBS 32 WOMAN

KERRI POMAROLLI

HARVEST HOUSE PUBLISHERS
EUGENE, OREGON

Cover design by Connie Gabbert Design + Illustration

Front cover photos © CSA-Printstock / iStockphoto ; Jullius / shutterstock

Cover Illustration by Connie Gabbert

Published in association with the literary agency of WordServe Literary Group, Ltd., www.wordserveliterary.com.

Where identifiable, people have given their permission for use of their name and stories.

Confessions of a Proverbs 32 Woman
Copyright © 2019 by Kerri Pomarolli
Published by Harvest House Publishers
Eugene, Oregon 97408
www.harvesthousepublishers.com

ISBN 978-0-7369-7748-7 (pbk.)
ISBN 978-0-7369-7749-4 (eBook)

Library of Congress Cataloging-in-Publication Data is on file at the Library of Congress, Washington, DC.

Printed in the United States of America
19 20 21 22 23 24 25 26 27 / BP-SK / 10 9 8 7 6 5 4 3 2 1

*This book is dedicated to everyone who saves
online recipes and never makes them.*

Acknowledgments

There are so many people to thank. If I forget to mention you here, you are probably in the book so keep reading.

First of all, God—for Proverbs 31 and the rest of the Bible.

My super agent, Greg Johnson, and super editor, Kathleen Kerr, and the nicest folks in publishing—my team at Harvest House.

My Mighty Women, My Wednesday morning ladies, Auntie Claire, Debbie, and Susie.

Tricia, who pored over my early drafts with love and corrected my grammar.

The Woman, Cathy, who has been in *all* of my books with wit and wisdom, who always takes my calls and doesn't charge me.

Gina, who also gives me free therapy and always encourages my healthy choices.

Mom and Dad, who keep my press releases going in Georgia to all their friends who diligently pray for me.

Uncle Mark, who takes my kids to movies so I can write.

And my darling children/tax write-offs, Lucy and Ruby, who are an unending source of material. Without you guys, Mommy would not have a career!

And to all the women who said, "Proverbs 32 Woman… not a bad idea!" This is for you!

Contents

Introduction

CONFESSION TIME

With two girls and a career of traveling around the country making people laugh, my life is far from "Insta-perfect." I live in LA, where all of the ultra-skinny people ask me if I'm pregnant. I started saying yes, since I look "good for four months preggo" (which I'm not).

I love God with my whole heart, but I skipped church the other day to watch VeggieTales. My kids eat raw veggies because their mom doesn't know how to steam them. They think a snack is a dirty Tic Tac from my purse.

You get the picture.

The truth is, I'm not the Proverbs 31 woman. Remember her? She's the perfect early-rising, field-plowing woman who makes her own clothes and has three jobs. I'm more like the Proverbs 32 woman. You haven't heard of her? Well, let me tell you. It's definitely me…and it's probably you if you're reading this book. These are our mantras:

"I will submit to *not* going to work!"

"I never pay retail."

"It's not gossip if your head is bowed!"

"Nutella solves all your problems." (And so does Ben and Jerry's.)

"We don't have issues. We have prayer requests."

However, if you're a type A, "got it together" girl, this book may send you into an OCD fit. You know who you are. Your boss loves you. If you have kids, they wear matching socks. You have Tupperware containers—with the lids on—neatly stacked and color coded in your kitchen. Good for you!

But if you are one of those women, then stop right now, slowly step away from the Kindle, and go make me some cookies in the shape of a rainbow. I need them for my kid's school tomorrow. And do you know how to make a fourth-grade science fair project by any chance?

But if you can relate to not being able to relate to that wonderful biblical woman of God that so few of us can actually measure up to, then buckle up! Because I'm about to convince you it is perfectly okay to be a #HotMess4Jesus.

Accepting that you are a Proverbs 32 Woman is the gift of being convinced that God is crazy about you. He completely understands you, loves you without complaint, passionately chases after you, and will never leave or forsake your hot-mess self for anything or anyone. You're loved. Safe. Accepted. Breathe deeply and smile. Get out that Nutella and eat some carbs! God created them. You can rest in the joy of being a Proverbs 32 Woman.

Accepting that you are a Proverbs 32 Woman is the gift of being convinced that God is crazy about you.

That is, if you can do two things.

First, you've got to be self-aware enough to admit who you are, where you are, and what you are. Really, this is the first key to loving your life and all the imperfections that seem to nag at your soul.

Second, you have to be God-aware enough to accept your Proverbs 32 Woman-ness with humility and grace. Embracing that it's okay not to have it all together—and not even caring whether you do or don't—brings a deep realization that Jesus is smiling over the very thought of you. When you can picture that love in His eyes, you can begin to grasp a firm and constant understanding of "how wide and long and high and deep is the love of Christ" (Ephesians 3:18)—especially for you.

Hot mess and all.

How do I know you can do this? I have the stories to prove it. And so do you, if you look deep enough. That's right: you can uncover the real you, look deep into your "hotmessness," and smile. You're just like the rest of the ladies at your church or at work—imperfect. Accept this gift of living in God's grace instead of condemnation, and then learn the secrets of giving this gift to your family, your friends, and perhaps even your mom! (Don't expect your mom to listen, though. I'm still working on mine.)

That's right: you can uncover the real you, look deep into your "hotmessness," and smile.

The chapters and stories that follow will take you on a wild ride through my very real life, no holds barred. They prove to me, and I hope they will prove to you, that this #hotmess4Jesus thing really can be the best possible life to live.

I'm not writing this book to solve your problems. There are enough of those kinds of books out there already. But if reading about my life can give you some comfort that you are not alone on this hamster wheel, then I've done my job. I promise, by the end of this book, you'll learn at least one thing: you are not the most messed-up chick in the room. I own that title!

Letter to the Proverbs 31 Woman

From: Kerri@proverbs32woman.com
To: Proverbs31woman@heaven.org
Subject: Heart on my sleeve

Dear Proverbs 31 Woman,

Hello, my name is Kerri. I found this email address for you on Twitter. (Did you know you have a Twitter account? Maybe you got hacked! Just let me know. I'll report it.)

I hope this email address works and this gets to you in heaven. I'm sure you're quite busy with all the fun festivities, but I wanted to introduce myself because I'm writing a book about you. Well, it's actually about me…but you inspired it. I wish I knew your name. May I call you Pearl? I would assume you have a beautiful holy name like that. My name means Dark Horse, but I'm sure my mom forgot to look that up before she picked out my name.

I'm here on earth, and I wanted to inform you that you've been inspiring women—and stressing them out—for centuries. You are an icon, and you have your very own chapter in the Holy Bible. A lot of women read about you in the Bible and think they could never measure up to all you were.

I have the utmost respect for you and all that you repre-sent. I just don't think I could be in your league. Nobody has ever called me a Proverbs 31 Woman. So I thought, *Why not embrace the reality that I'm more a Proverbs 32 Woman and see how we can support each other?* I hope we can bridge the gap for all women, whether they are Proverbs 31 or 32. We are all precious in His sight, created in His image. And when I say "precious," I don't mean it in a patronizing way, like, "Oh, your baby is so adorable even though he has no hair!" I mean God loves each and every one of us.

> ## *Why not embrace the reality that I'm more a Proverbs 32 Woman and see how we can support each other?*

I'm writing this book to help the woman out there who isn't feeling so great about herself. I hope she will read it and realize the truth about how much God loves her, right where she is. He's not waiting for her to be ten pounds lighter, ten years younger, or ten dollars richer. He loves all His kids exactly where they are—we can't do anything to make Him love us any more, and we can't do anything to make Him love us any less.

Did you ever have early mornings when you lie in bed, afraid to open your eyes? I can get pretty overwhelmed thinking about the demands waiting for me as soon as my feet hit the floor, and in some cases, before my feet hit the floor. Right now it's 5:20 a.m. and I'm awake. At any given moment a child is going to come running into my room, insisting that I fetch things for her, as though I am her servant. You had kids, but you also had servants. That might be something I need to look into.

Some days...okay, *most* days lately...I want to be a kid again. I want to go back to the time when my mom would stick a thermometer in my mouth, put a hot compress on my head, and tell me to stay in bed for the rest of the day. She would let me watch *The Price Is Right* and *I Love Lucy* and she would feed me Ritz Crackers and Campbell's chicken noodle soup. (I'm pretty sure those cubes were not chicken.) Then in the afternoon I would lie on the couch while she did Jazzercise and watched her "stories" (*General Hospital*). Then she would make Stove Top Stuffing and some vegetable from a Green Giant for dinner, and I wouldn't have a care in the world. My dad would read a story to me and kiss me good night while I was snuggled under my covers wearing my pink flannel Precious Moments nightgown, and he would bring me a Coke to settle my stomach. Sometimes, if it was Friday night, I would get to fall asleep watching *The Golden Girls* in my mom's bed.

But now I'm the mom, and I don't have anyone to kiss me on the forehead and tuck me in at night. I'm expected to do all those things for other people. And how do they thank me? They pee in my bed!

I just don't want to do any adulting today! It's too hard. I can't believe I'm a grown-up. When did that happen? I mean, my friends and I own houses that look like the ones we grew up in. When I'm invited to a barbecue, it still boggles my mind that I'm the one who is supposed to take the food. Isn't that a grown-up's job? I can't work a grill!

I feel ill-equipped for so much in this life. I wish I could have been more prepared. Instead of learning Algebra 2, maybe my math teacher could have taught me how to do online banking. Or what about changing a flat tire or folding a fitted sheet? I have to do all the work, all the time, and it's a thankless job, let me tell you. And I get up each day and it starts all over again.

I'm tired, Pearl. I'm really, truly tired. No cream, ointment, pill, or anything else I've purchased online seems to help on days like this. Did you ever just want to pack up the camel and get out of town? By yourself? Did ever get any alone time?

What were your biggest worries? After you read my book, you might think I worry a lot. But I like to call it "verbal processing." I just like to rant about things to make myself feel better. What did you do to comfort yourself on hard days? I can only imagine how difficult your struggles were compared to my issues (I mean prayer requests). Though you did have servants to help. I'm kind of envious of that. I'd settle for a cleaning person once a month!

Did the servants tend to the children? Or did they do the water runs and plow the field? It seems you were quite crafty, making garments and selling them. You would do very well today on a thing called Etsy. We don't have a watering hole, but women gather on social media. It's not the same as connecting face-to-face—our faces are photoshopped anyway—and we feel more disconnected from the world than ever. I can tell you what my best friend had for dinner last night, but I haven't heard her voice on the phone, seen her face, or given her a hug in a very long time. I miss that. I miss talking to friends and doing life with my tribe. Now I just look at pictures of their lives. I miss having close friends who talk openly and honestly.

I'm sure you had good fellowship time. And I hear the men made it a point to sit at the city gate, including your husband. Was he working there or what? I mean, were you the breadwinner? Not that it's a bad thing. I'm a single mom and I'm responsible for myself and these two other humans who keep calling me mom. Sometimes I fear what would become of them if something happened to me. That fear keeps me up at night.

Did you sleep well? I bet you were exhausted. I don't sleep that well sometimes. Usually around one o'clock in the morning, my brain turns on a slide show of pictures of all the problems and ideas that demand my attention. Currently I'm working on building a weight-loss plan: how to lose ten pounds while eating bread but without doing any extra physical activity. I love bread. I could have lived on manna for 40 years if I had some avocados and lemon juice.

But if I'm really putting my heart on my sleeve, what I am hoping, maybe, even after reading about all my dysfunction, is that you will consider being my friend. No pressure. Thank you for taking the time to read this.

Your friend (hopefully),
Kerri

P.S. Who is the best person you've met up there? Any surprises? Could you check and see if someone named Patrick Swayze is there? He'd probably be teaching the praise dance at the campgrounds with King David. Oh, and while you're at it, my mom wants you to look for a guy named Clark Gable. I don't think he'd be dancing.

QUIZ: ARE YOU A
PROVERBS 31 OR PROVERBS 32 WOMAN?

1. Do you rise early, and does anyone call you "blessed" before 8:00 a.m.?

2. Do you plow?

3. Do you avoid "the bread of idleness"? Have you ever taken a nap in the daytime?

4. Do you own a spindle? And do you use it on a regular basis to make clothes of scarlet?

5. Do you quilt or make your own bedding because you won't set foot in a TJ Maxx or HomeGoods?

6. Are you the owner of any fields or vineyards?

7. Do you have a Pinterest page of things you've actually made in real life? Do you sell linen garments on Etsy?

8. Does farm-to-table organic fermenting of foods sound fun to you?

9. Does it sound wrong for you to even think about serving produce out of a can with a Green Giant on the label? Or lasagna from an orange box?

10. Would you consider it a bad thing to eat Nutella in the shower, fully clothed, with a fork?

Scoring

If you answered yes to 3 or more of the above questions, you are a Proverbs 31 Woman. You are definitely getting a mega mansion in heaven and a *huge* crown with massive jewels. A spot is waiting for you, and you will be on the kitchen committee with Martha. You are someone who can "laugh at days to come" and "be praised." I suggest you buy my Proverbs 32 Woman devotional, because you are going to need to learn how to help the rest of us.

If you answered no to 5 or more questions, there is no doubt: you are a Proverbs 32 Woman! Welcome to the club! You need to find a Proverbs 31 woman to mentor you. She will make your birthday cakes and joyfully decorate any of your tables for women's events. She can also help you sew your kids' costumes for the Christmas pageant, even at the last minute when you find out the night before that your child has been cast as a shepherd. You love variety in life, and you appreciate the value of Uber Eats delivery. You do your quiet time of reflection at HomeGoods. As a Proverbs 32 Woman, you should also get my new devotional because you will find our sisterhood is bigger than you think. You are not alone. We all need each other…and chocolate. There was definitely chocolate in the garden of Eden.

1

JAZZ CLASS GROUPON

really did it this time. I blame Groupon.

In my infinite wisdom, I decided to take a jazz class last night. Jazz class is a happy part of my childhood, and I guess I signed up on a day when I was feeling rather good about myself, in that "I can fit into my skinny jeans so I can conquer the world" kind of way. I'd been dieting like a mad woman for this ridiculous high school reunion. I tried on the sequined outfit I wore to the last reunion…and it fit! I mean, it really fit. Not just in that way where you have to hold your breath.

But just because the jeans fit doesn't necessarily mean we should move on to the Lycra and the leg warmers that have been under the bed for ten years. But no one told me this, so I suited up and went to the dance studio. The sign should have been my first clue that this wasn't going to be exactly what I expected. The studio was called Celestial Expressions, and the girl on the billboard looked more like a Gumby rubber toy than a dancer.

Just because the jeans fit doesn't
necessarily mean we should move on
to the Lycra and the leg warmers that
have been under the bed for ten years.

Here's how it went:

> **Tammy, the Perky Desk Clerk:** Hello, can I help you?
> (So, obviously she thought I was a Mary Kay salesperson
> and in no way was I there to take a jazz class.)
>
> **Me:** I'm here for the class.
>
> **Tammy:** What class?
>
> **Me:** The jazz class at 7:00 p.m.
>
> **Tammy (with a look of terror on her face as she tried to
> hide her horror at my parachute pants):** "Ohhhhh, I'm
> sorry. Studio A. Right down the hall. Tiffany Amber Jas-
> mine will be with you in five minutes as soon as she's done
> with her charcoal ice cream."

Since the teacher's name was Tiffany Amber Jasmine, I could
assume she'd just graduated from twelfth grade, at best. If the teacher
was named Madame Olga, Dawn, or Jennifer, then there was a fighting chance she would be close to my age. But not Tiffany. Tiffanies are
cute and perky. They wear bouncing ponytails, chew pink bubble gum,
eat pasta for dinner, and never gain an ounce.

I walked into the studio, and there were *literally* three girls there.
When I say girls, I mean girls…as in high school. They were in a hud-
dle discussing the trauma of their school's new policy on uniforms, and
they were very worried about how tenth grade was going to be much

more demanding than ninth. The tall girl in the middle looked my way with an expression that seemed to say, "Haven't I babysat for one of your kids?"

They continued their conversation without including me, so I sat down on the floor and searched for my phone so I could look popular. Thankfully I hadn't yet deleted Facebook from my phone (yes, I eventually did that, but more on that later), and I immediately went to my safe place, since I'm very well-liked on Facebook. That is why I carry my phone with me everywhere, in case of moments like these.

I heard one of them say to the others, "I know, it's, like, um, so on point 'cause I, like, um, get to do the thing, like, every day." The other girls who spoke her language nodded in total agreement, understanding every word she said.

After nine unbearably long minutes, Tiffany ("I'm so beautiful and skinny and I eat cupcakes for breakfast with my organic kale açai smoothie and weigh 104") walked in. She was clearly old. And by old, I mean 20. She said, "Okay, guys, welcome to jazz basic. I'm Tiff, and we're going to do a lot of floor work and turns and leaps tonight. Let's start our warm-up with an oldie but goodie."

I was thinking she'd play Michael Jackson, or maybe my man Prince. But then she turned on a Beyoncé song. (So apparently Beyoncé is really old now. If you come out with a hit song and then you have a baby, you are put out into pop culture oblivion. Unless your name is Madonna.)

The music was playing and all four of us jazz divas were doing the warm-up. Except that my muscles hadn't done any warm-ups like those in literally ten years. I used to dance. I used to be somebody! I used to be a contender! When I took classes back in the day, I'd see these moms sneaking into my classes, all with their Fosse jazz hands, trying to keep up. Back then, in NYC at Steps Studio, I'd say to myself, "May I never be like one of those old ladies in their (gasp!) thirties." Then I'd laugh with my six-pack abs flexing in my dish towel of a top!

My mom was a Jazzercise diva in her day, and I remember judging her too. "May I never be like my mother, Barbara, who dragged me to her Jazzercise classes where I sat on the floor eating Cheerios and watching middle-aged women run in place singing 'Maniac' on the dance floor." And in case that's not enough of a mental picture, it gets worse. You should have seen them wagging their hips and marching in place, singing, "I Will Survive!" by Donna Summer. These images are burned into the memories of my childhood.

So there I was, now the mom doing my best to look cool. As I looked at these tenth graders wearing the same rainbow leg warmers I had in high school, it hit me that the new dancewear styles are throwbacks to the '80s and '90s, so I actually did fit right in, at least in the wardrobe department. (So here's a tip for you: never throw anything away; just put it under the bed for at least ten years. It will come back in style.)

The warm-up was difficult. It's hard to explain, but let me try to give you a visual. Tiffany was lifting one leg up high by her ear while standing. I imagined she was a Twister national champion. She then asked us to show her our center splits. Center splits? That is not natural. My legs hadn't been in that position since the last time I gave birth. And as the mother of two daughters, I knew that if I attempted this position, I just might pee on myself. Still, I couldn't be shown up by the young'uns. So I spread my legs as far as they would go…and then I got stuck. I was not in the splits, but I was not standing up either. I was exactly smack-dab in the middle, forming some kind of crooked V with my legs, and I couldn't move. I couldn't get up or roll over. My hamstrings were cramping with the worst charley horse pain you can imagine.

I didn't want anyone to know. The other girls were fully and comfortably stretched into their split positions. (I'd like to see them go through the births of two kids and give it a try then.) I used my arms to try to push my legs harder and wider apart, and that's when I audibly heard the tendons in my thighs ripping to shreds. I realized at this point that I was not going any farther down. So I used my arms to grab on to each thigh and pull myself up to safety, all while waving my jazz hands and sparkle fingers.

I used my arms to grab on to each thigh and pull myself up to safety, all while waving my jazz hands and sparkle fingers.

Tiffany was very clued into my difficulty and tried not to draw any attention to me, for which I was grateful. The question on her face seemed to ask, "Do we need an ambulance?" But she just nodded at me and said, "Um…do as much as you can!"

Do as much as you can? *Do as much as you can?* Do you know what that means? It means, "Don't overdo it, old lady, because when you fall and break a hip, I don't want to get sued. And I don't know why you're even here in the first place. You should probably go to Jazzercise."

I just smiled and kept my hips moving from side to side, like I was working on a new move.

I wasn't about to be outdone by the Teen Squad. It was time for leaps and turns across the floor. Here was my chance. I used to rock this! I knew I had it in me, and the first round wasn't half bad. I did some leaping and turning, and I didn't even fall down. Did I experience extreme vertigo? Yes, of course. Did the room seem to spin in 14 directions, causing me to feel like I had just ridden Space Mountain at Disneyland? Yes, absolutely. Did I have to focus with great intensity just to walk in a straight line back to my spot? Yes, but I did it! Mission accomplished! No falling! And no blood!

Unfortunately, for the next go across the floor, I was feeling overly confident. Have you ever heard of Mikhail Baryshnikov? I think, in that moment, I thought I was him. I thought I'd add a little split into my leaps, so I geared up like an Olympic athlete. With jazz fingers spread and eyes focused, I did a few runs. I thrust my legs into the air and attempted a scissors-type motion before landing. *Attempted* is the key word in this sentence. I know I should give myself an A for effort, but I also know my legs hadn't tried to do anything like this maneuver, um, ever. And so, instead of scissor-kicking, my muscles rebelled. They decided to set their own personal boundary. I stopped mid-air and landed on the ground with a loud *thud*.

Luckily, Lady Gaga was loud enough on the boom box to drown out the sound of my elephant landing. I just smiled and sashayed back to my place. With each additional run across the floor, I gave it my all. I was a maniac on that dance floor for sure! *Flashdance* had nothing on me.

I looked at the clock, and it was time for class to be over. Our lovely, energetic teacher said, "You guys are so awesome. Let's go another 15 minutes, okay?" Well, of course I had to stay and torture myself. She put us through some more combinations and across-the-floor moves. I did every single one without bleeding. It was like an out-of-body experience. My mind was saying, "Yes, you can do this!" and my body was saying, "Please don't make me do this!"

When class was over I collected my things and what was left of my dignity, and I hobbled to the car. As I walked into the house that night, I said to my family, "Kids, tonight Mommy was a rock star dancer!"

And then I fell onto the couch and said, "Can somebody get me the Bengay?"

Okay, I'm not sure I have found some deep spiritual lesson in the whole dance class experience, but it definitely showed me how big God's sense of humor is. I could hear Him laughing at me from heaven! He gave me my love of dancing when I was three years old, so He must have a perfect place for me to express it. Maybe the perfect place is in the privacy of my own home, doing dance parties in my living room with my girls.

I wonder if they had dance parties in Bible times. I mean, from what I hear, King David was a dancing maniac too. Did you hear about the time his wife bawled him out after he was literally "Dancin' in the Streets"? Can you blame her? I heard he was naked!

I also wonder if the Proverbs 31 Woman worked out. Maybe she didn't have to, since her whole life was physical labor. I think she had to walk six miles each way, just to get water. Anyway, all the clothes in the Bible sound pretty baggy, so maybe it didn't matter to her if she was fat or thin. Funny, God never talks much about fitness in the Bible. He just says that our body is a temple. And, as one of my comedian friends used to deadpan, "I'm building a megachurch!"

But I only get one go-around in this life, and as long as God gives me a healthy body, I'm gonna work it. It's good to challenge ourselves and do things that scare us. We get busy with life, jobs, relationships, and kids, but there's no time like the present to do the things we've been meaning to do. I had been meaning to go to a class like that for a long time and I finally did it. I'm glad I tried.

**It's good to challenge ourselves
and do things that scare us.**

Maybe I'll take another dance class in the future, since I found one called "Dance It Out—for Baby Boomers." It sounds like it's just my speed and style. There is only one problem...it's at the Senior Citizen Center, and I'll have to get a fake ID that says I'm 55 to get in. Now, you probably think I'm joking about that. But they literally told me I couldn't come to the boomers' class because I'm not old enough. So I'm too old for hip-hop jazz, and now I'm too young for boomers. Once again I feel like a square peg in a round hole. I suppose you could say that's been the theme of my life—never fitting in.

I used to make fun of comedians who did age jokes. I promised myself I'd never become one of those "old ladies" longing for yesteryear. But here I am…Pot…Kettle…Black. And maybe it's a question I need to ask myself. Am I okay with the age I am and the body I have? Okay, probably every woman reading this just shouted, "Nooooooo!"

I get you. I'm with you. I live in LA where no one ages. They just get Botox—and fillers and liposuction and face lifts. I mean, seriously, even Betty White's forehead is smooth. So it's strange that I never thought about aging until this recent experience. Most of the time I don't feel like I'm a day over 25 (although at this precise moment my body feels like I could check myself into an assisted living facility and they'd take me, no questions asked). I still sometimes feel as though I should be able to do everything I could do when I was 20, with the same amount of ease. After all, we see celebrities every single day who are fighting a battle against Father Time quite splendidly—and winning! And they also promise us that we can look exactly like them if we buy their skincare products and workout equipment. We also forget they are mostly airbrushed in the photographs of them doing their "yogalates" and "cardio barre." The only exceptions are Cindy Crawford, Sophia Loren, and of course Robert Downey Jr. But they are immortal.

The question I have for myself and for you is: How can I find balance between being okay with who I am right now and still wanting to take on new challenges? I mean, it doesn't sound as if the women in the Bible worried about aging. They mostly lived to be over 100, and some of them were even bearing children in those years. (When my daughter asked me for a little brother years ago, I told her I was too old. She replied, "No way, Mom! Sarah was 80 when she had her first kid!" All that Bible school backfires on me every so often.)

I want to learn from the women in the Bible, but I also realize we are living in a totally different society. They were worried about literal survival in the face of famines and boils and plagues. They were happy to live to see another birthday. I'm worried about getting thinner thighs and trying to do a center split to impress girls I could have given birth to.

And speaking of the girls I actually did give birth to, my two daughters seem to like me just fine the way I am. They crawl in bed with me, and they tell me I'm the most cuddly mama in the world. I don't think I would be so cuddly if I were as thin as the models in magazines. They just look angry and hungry.

Whose approval am I really searching for? Mine? God's? My family's and friends'? All of the above, I suppose. I need to pare that list down to the basics. God gave me this body that, by His grace, gets up and walks and talks and drives and dances and functions, for the most part quite nicely. He also gave me the desire to bust a move every once in a while.

So I think I'm going to continue the tradition in my house that we like to call "Holy Spirit Dance Party." We put on some Kirk Franklin praise music and jam out in my living room. It burns calories and teaches my kids that Christian music can be cool and funky too. (Oh, snap! Did I just actually write the word *funky*? As in Marky Mark and the Funky Bunch? Yes, it's official—I am 105. But I look gooood for that age, girl!)

Hey, that reminds me of what my mother always told me: "The older we say we are, the better we look for our age!"

So what about you? Got any secret desire to try something crazy and fun? (Did I inspire or scare you? Maybe both?) Have you ever wanted to do something crazy but were too afraid of what others would think?

No matter how you feel, I hope you will think of me the next time you get out there and "Jam on It"!

And now, if you'll excuse me, I have to go ice my thighs.

2

22 MINUTES

ere's the story. I booked a comedy gig that turned out to be an outdoor event held in a tent on the sweatiest day of the summer. I flew to Oakland, California, with my crew, including my two little roadies, Lucy and Ruby, to do comedy in a tent for a church's groundbreaking celebration. It felt very biblical, like an old-time revival, except for the fact that it was 95 degrees and people in our audience were passing out from heat exhaustion and drinking Mountain Dew and eating funnel cakes and churros and my comedy was competing with the tractor pull competition on the other side of the field.

Because moms rarely get to choose the battleground, my daughter Lucy chose that day of all days for an epic battle of wills. Earlier that day she had been acting inappropriately, as I like to call it. I told her that her punishment was no sweet treats for the rest of the day because she was not behaving like a lady (she threw a tantrum right in front of the ladies' room). And then I walked right up to a booth, ordered the biggest blue raspberry snow cone they made, and ate it in front of my kid. Call me a mean mom or call me brilliant. I knew we were going to be at this fair, surrounded by carnival foods, and she needed to learn a lesson in the school of hard knocks. She was fuming mad, but like her mother, she is not one to go down without a fight.

She promptly looked right at me and said, "Well, Mommy, you're right. I didn't want all that sugar anyway. You told me it rots my teeth, and it isn't good for me. I'd rather go to the petting zoo. Thanks, Mommy, this was a great punishment!"

Are you kidding me? Who is this kid, and where are her parents?

I got played by my own kid. At first I was mad at her manipulation, and then dollar signs flashed in my head as I considered what a great lawyer she'll make someday (or perhaps she'll be a dictator of a small country). My relationship with Lucy is all about trying to make the world a safer place by harnessing her powers for good, not evil. She now tells me she wants to be a Supreme Court justice because "they can never fire me!"

Still, watching my girl melt down at the worst time reminded me that my life, like yours, can be a bit out of control. Do you have time to breathe, relax, or even squeeze God into your margins? Maybe you can relate to how I was feeling. Such is my life. And honestly, it's a good one right now.

Do you have time to breathe, relax, or even squeeze God into your margins?

Why did I say "right now," you ask?

Well, because I'm not in the middle of any major crisis. And when there's a chance to come up for air, I take it. I'm trying to learn to live in the "right now"—not the yesterdays or tomorrows. I've wasted too many hours of my life figuring out the best- and worst-case scenarios for whatever trial I thought I might face. Right now, in this moment, nothing is threatening my life or the lives of the people I love, and that hasn't always been true. So I'm trying to breathe in the "right now" and discover what peace feels like.

I seem to have lived my adult life—and maybe even my childhood, if I'm really honest—on high alert. Yes, there have been incredible moments along the way, but sometimes I feel as though I've been skipping stones above the waters of insanity. I think that's why I've always clung to the promise in Isaiah 43:2: "When you pass through the rivers, they will not sweep over you." I need that promise when it feels as if the water is right up to my nose.

People say to me—*all* the time—that old cliché: "I don't know how you do it, Kerri. You've gone through so much with all of the illnesses and struggles in your family. It's amazing you're still here. You're so strong." I guess their intention is to make me feel better, but all I can hear is the reminder that I've gone through a lot of painful stuff. I realize my friends are speaking the truth, but I wish they could tell by the look on my face that I'm not in a place to receive it at the moment. As we say in comedy, "Know your audience!"

People also say stuff like, "To whom much is given, much will be required." Or the ever popular, "You must be doing something right because all this is coming against you."

Really, people? Really?

I want to wear a sign for all the well-meaning do-gooders in my life that says,

---

Hello, friend. I'm going through something right now. Here's what I don't need, unless I ask for it:

1. Your opinion on how to fix my problems.

2. Any words you've found on a Hallmark card or a Susan Polis Schutz inspirational calendar.

3. Any Internet nonsense forwarded to my Inbox

with instructions to forward to a dozen other people, lest bad luck befall my home and worse things happen to me.

4. Inspirational magnets you bought at Cracker Barrel.

Here's what I do need:

1. Cash.

2. Casseroles.

3. Your prayers for me. Like, for real. Don't just say you're going to pray. (I do that all the time, but I try to keep my word. I have to write their name on my hand, literally, so I don't forget!)

I've definitely had my fair share of "walking through the water just trying not to drown" seasons in my life. Some days I feel as though Satan's got a dartboard with my picture on it. I wish I didn't feel that way. I know I'm nobody special, but it seems as though I'm always walking through something major. When it isn't me, it's someone in my family, and it seems no one in my immediate circle has been immune to Satan's dumb attacks. There's a TV show called *The Walking Dead*, and my family could be called "The Walking Wounded." The characters on that show die a thousand times and keep going, kind of like my family with all we've been through. My mother has had over 25 surgeries, and she's had breast cancer three times. And that's just for starters. It'd be a whole other book if I told you all the trials we've faced in the health department.

But I have to remember this: all of us are still standing. We're not dead, and we didn't roll over like Satan wanted us to. We know how to fight. Being Italian helps too.

I get the honor of going places and meeting people nearly every week. I tell them about the battles I've faced, and I encourage them that God will come through for them. I definitely hear hundreds and hundreds of women's stories about what they're facing, and it would be enough to make me lose sleep at night if I didn't believe there is a God up there who cares about each of their needs.

I was at a prayer meeting the other night with some awesome ladies. These are the kind of prayer warriors you want on your side in any battle. They could call down fire from heaven and not think it was a big deal. I'm talking literal fire! My friend Nicki had gathered us all in one place for some serious prayer time. I didn't know all of them, but when it was my turn to receive prayer, they all laid their hands on me and prayed for me. I have to admit something: it was the first time in a long while that I had people lay hands on me.

Right now I'm in an in-between place. I'm not in the middle of a crisis where I'm down on my face doing the ugly cry, and I'm not in total victory where I feel healed from all the carnage and battle wounds that come from spiritually duking it out with Satan himself. Honestly, I just want to be left alone. I feel like I'm in a "duck and cover" spiritual season.

When these sweet prayer ladies started praying for me, I couldn't sit still. I felt like my daughter Ruby when she's trying to sit through big people's church. I was attempting to look focused, but my mind was running to a million other places. I kept wanting to get up for snacks. (By the way, Nicki always has the best snacks. And we both know you can't have a prayer meeting without a cheese tray, right?) I knew I needed some prayer and support, and there were things in my life I wanted straightened out. But I hadn't taken the time to talk to God about myself in so long. I was too busy putting on my spiritual war paint and going into battle for everyone else—my kids, my parents, my friends, and the countless people I had heard about from friends and random strangers.

If someone needs prayer, I'll be the first one to step up to the plate. But when it came to God and me personally, I had dropped the ball and I didn't even realize it. As I felt the weight of their hands and their words, I realized I hadn't been spending much time with God at all. And I mean *not at all*!

My friend Victoria said, ever so boldly and calmly, "You need to let us pray for you to feel God's love. Go sit on your Papa God's lap and let Him comfort your heart. You know there are places in your heart that still need healing, Kerri. Only He can mend those broken places. Jesus wants you to feel how very much He loves you. Not the version of you we see on stage, and not the version of you who's helping everybody all the time. He loves you apart from what you do or how you do it. When you feel His presence, you can be at a place of rest, no matter what is going on around you."

In my mind, all I kept thinking was, *Oh, for the love, are we digging up old wounds again? I can't handle this. I'm going to run out of here. I wonder what's on Netflix right now? Wait, is that Brie on the cheese tray?*

Has that ever happened to you? Have you listened to someone pray for you, all the while feeling distracted by the pressure to have this big "God revelation moment" when you feel nothing? Yep, that was me.

So when she asked me if I wanted to pray for God to speak to me right then and there, I couldn't do it. I was too nervous and afraid it wouldn't happen. I knew I'd be stuck and embarrassed that I couldn't hear God. I knew where the problem was, and I didn't want to admit to them I had been too busy for God. So I just asked them to pray that God would show me how to feel His presence in His own way. And then I ate a wheel of cheese and crackers and some grapes.

Can I be honest with you? I really want to spend time with God, but here's what my mornings look like—my real morning, not the one on Instagram. I wake up at 6:00 a.m. to my daughter Ruby wanting to "play worship," which means I'm supposed to get out of bed to get her flags down so she can loudly sing and dance around my house. Who am I to stop her? She's worshiping! I make breakfast, which consists of whatever I can find that resembles healthy food (usually an egg if I'm feeling gourmet). I shove vitamins in my daughters' mouths and recite a Bible verse with them because I'm a spiritual giant…and that counts as my quiet time, right?

There's very little margin. Very little. Did I check my "Verse for the Day" on my cell phone? Sure! Wow! I'm so spiritual. Yes, I have a million books about God and prayer, and my bedside table is filled with articles about spiritual warfare. But who has time to read? And in all of this I had left out the most important ingredient: God loving me.

God sent His only Son down to earth to teach us about love, first and foremost. Everything else comes after that. I wish I could say I was so much better about spending time with God before marriage or kids, but I'd be lying. You've probably heard of a type A personality, but I'm a type AAA, basically from birth. I was always the kid who couldn't sit still, and I became the adult who made multitasking an Olympic sport. So I can't blame this busyness on motherhood or the life stage I'm in right now. The truth is I've struggled with this whole "quiet time with God" thing my entire life. And I know I need to do better, but will I? Is it too late to change?

God sent His only Son down to earth to teach us about love, first and foremost. Everything else comes after that.

That night at Nicki's, after I had consumed a cow's worth of cheese, when it was time to pray for another one of my friends, it was like my spirit immediately woke up. Once I was out of the hot seat, I was on fire! I was proclaiming victory and truth, praying for my captive friend to be set free. With a sword in my hand, I was no longer fidgety. I was comfortable in warrior position. I was focused, right on task, praying to see God come through and be glorified in my friend's circumstance. I could have continued in this prayer for hours, and it would have seemed like minutes. But this warrior posture is totally different from the resting place Victoria had described earlier, and I knew it. Warriors don't sit still, but they do need to rest between battles. I realized if I didn't find a way to rest soon, I was going to crash and burn and be no good to anyone.

I knew I had to rush home that night to prepare to take an early-morning flight the following day to minister to a bunch of ladies. I drove home late, packed my suitcase, and crashed into bed at about midnight, knowing I had to catch a taxi at 5:30 the next morning. On the night before a trip, I have this tradition with Lucy, my oldest: I steal her from her bed when she's sleeping and put her in bed with me. But on that night I forgot. I was just too tired. I passed out, spent and exhausted.

At about 4:30 a.m., I saw this little shadow at my bedroom door. Lucy said, "Mama, can I come cuddle with you? Just for a few minutes? Because I...I...um...I miss you already."

Of course my heart broke into a million pieces when I looked into that little face with one tear streaming down her rosy cheek. You would have had to carry me away from her with a forklift to make me leave her in that moment. She came into bed, cuddled up in my arms, and immediately fell fast asleep with the cutest smile of contentment I'd ever seen. She was safe in her mama's arms. She was at peace.

Knowing I had to be out of the bed in 22 minutes, I kept looking at her, then closing my eyes, then glancing again at the red numbers on the alarm clock. I kept brushing her hair and kissing her little precious head. As the minutes ticked away, I'd squeeze her a little tighter. I couldn't get enough of her, and I knew my time with her was short.

I don't get moments like this with Lucy much anymore because she runs around like a Tasmanian devil every hour she is awake (and I mean that in the most flattering way). She's typically climbing trees or raiding my cabinets and making explosions of homemade slime in my kitchen. But in those fleeting moments, when I could actually feel her breathing, I experienced the most satisfying feeling. I didn't want it to end. But I knew I only had minutes left, and they were slipping away from me fast.

As I looked at my daughter one last time that morning, I could hear the unmistakable voice inside my spirit, the voice of my Father God. He said to me, "My little bumblebee, Kerri, as you hold your daughter and breathe in the very essence of her being, feeling as though your time together is going much too fast, just know, My little darling, this is exactly how I feel about you. I love you so much, and I long to have you lay here in My arms and let Me hold you. I can bring you the peace you long for. I can comfort your soul. Just give Me some undistracted time. Stop being too busy for Me. I want you to need Me when times are good, not just when you're desperate. I love you so much. Take a minute from all your buzzing around, working to make all that honey, to land in My arms."

As the tears welled up in my eyes, the conviction felt like a hot knife in my chest. God would have been happy with 22 minutes of my time on those days when I was rushing around trying to save the world all by myself. He wasn't mad at me. He wasn't even disappointed in me. He was just so in love with His daughter that He missed her. He missed me: Kerri. Not Hollywood comedian, minister, mom…just me.

I wanted to tell Him I was so sorry. I wanted to crawl up into His arms and ask Him to help me slow down. I keep getting back on this hamster wheel, and I can't do life alone. I have to remember that all of the things I think are so vital to get done will go ever so much more smoothly if I allow God to get involved.

But one thing I have learned is that my old friends, Guilt and Condemnation, are just as big of a hindrance as all the other distractions. The enemy wants us to feel horrible and condemned so we'll become paralyzed and afraid to make a move in any direction, much less toward God. The enemy wants us to wallow in our self-defeat so we'll feel unworthy of being loved by anybody, much less God our Father.

But that moment in bed, curled up with my daughter, I had a sudden awareness. I realized I was on the crazy cycle, and it was up to me to get off. This was just as big a battle as any others, but I had to find a different way to fight.

And so I did. In the days that followed, I made an effort to care for my soul, to intentionally do the things I knew would be beneficial for my spirit. If God wanted more time with me, He knew it was for my own good. But I needed to make some space to see Him in my day.

God didn't move. I did.

I immediately deleted my Facebook and social media apps off my phone. That was the only way they weren't going to take over my day. If I really need to visit those sites, I can do it from my home computer. I don't need the apps following me around, buzzing with notifications and begging for my attention.

I started putting on worship music in my house, and I've learned to keep it going all day. I've never been drawn to long periods of musical worship. I get bored with all that singing. I'm a warrior more than a worshiper, which is likely part of my problem. But for this experiment, putting on worship music was essentially a battle cry. If I'm playing worship music while doing other things, I'm still connected to the Holy Spirit. It's the best kind of multitasking. I even put reminders on my phone twice a day that say, "Kerri, put on worship music in your house." Because, as my grandmama used to say, "The good Word drives the devil out of the house!" It can't hurt, right?

I also began looking up some of my favorite Bible teachers and watching their videos on YouTube. Hey, it's better than dancing kittens or all the other viral stuff I let clog my brain. (Except for the military reunions. I can't get enough of those!)

I've also been making an effort to pray while I am sitting still. And then after I pray, I try to sit still for a few minutes to just listen to God. I got out one of those journals that's been sitting by my bed, and I take the time to write down my feelings. Journaling may not be your thing, but when I journal, I write letters to God. It's actually really awesome. I pour out my soul to Him. I tell Him my fears, and I also tell Him I know He will take care of me. Then I feel at peace, ready to attack anything the day brings.

I've been making it a point to read my Bible, no matter what. Sometimes I read it out loud. (I know I won't fall asleep that way.) Sometimes I read it over a few times to let it sink in. There is no perfect way to read your Bible, but I can tell you that this focus for the past few weeks has given me more peace each day to face the grenades the world throws at me.

All these practices didn't seem overwhelming once I got into the groove of them. And it all started when God asked me for just 22 minutes. For some of you that can seem like a lifetime of being still. But I promise: if you give it a chance, it will be life changing.

When you're feeling stressed out and wound up, you can follow these three easy steps.

1. *Focus.* Take away anything that might distract you when you're trying to spend time with God. Remove phones, magazines, cleaning tools, or whatever pulls your attention away from your focus on God. Set a timer for 22 minutes, and commit to connecting your spirit with God—*no matter what*. It will get easier the more you do it. And don't beat yourself up if 22 minutes seems impossible for you. Maybe start with waking up 5 to 10 minutes early, or take some time before you go to bed to reflect on your day. I keep some Scripture cards right by my bed. They are short and easy affirmations that God loves me, reminding me I am more than enough.

**Set a timer for 22 minutes,
and commit to connecting your
spirit with God—*no matter what*.**

---

2. *Praise.* Turn on praise music in your home and see how you feel. Does it uplift you—and maybe even your family? Have a praise dance party! You still got moves, girl! And it counts as a workout. I highly recommend Kirk Franklin, but then again, "Livin' on a Prayer" has a good message too. No, I'm not kidding.

3. *Pray.* When you take time to pray to God, stop for a few minutes and listen. Grab a journal if that helps. And do what I do: ask God to yell loudly. My journals used to be filled with pages about all my boyfriends. Now they are filled with my letters to God. Journaling is a way to really get to the bottom of what I'm dealing with that day— good, bad, or ugly. (Just make sure your journal has a lock on it. My kids are stealthy and sneaky, and yours probably are too.)

Just remember F.P.P. This can also stand for french fries, potato chips, and pancakes. Those are all spiritual too! And, finally, know this: you're going to be just fine!

3

MY NINE-YEAR-OLD IS WAY MORE CHRISTIAN THAN I AM

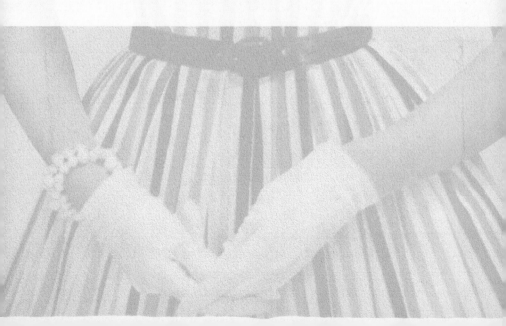

'll admit it: I struggle with finding that elusive, coveted "Bible time with my blessed Savior," as the saints call it. I could blame the fact that I have two kids, a full-time job, and a number of other things, but I'd be lying. I've struggled with reading my Bible since...well, since I could read my Bible.

If you ask me to attend a prayer meeting for four hours, I'm your girl. If someone needs comfort and biblical encouragement, look no further—I've got you! But ask me to sit by myself in a room with a Bible, and I might make it three minutes before I'm overtaken by the urge to check Facebook to see who likes my new haircut or to find slow-cooker recipes that use Cheez Whiz. It's like a physical pull. I start reading Psalm 23, and suddenly I'm on Pinterest looking at "How to Paint Your Entryway Stairs in Rustic Fall Colors!" (You guys, I don't even have stairs in my house.) Then a coupon from Cost Plus World Market pops up on my phone and I'm a goner.

I know this is ridiculous. But I also know I'm not the only one. Admit it, you're reading this right now while surfing Amazon for the perfect new bedspread. I've even had the compulsion to clean instead of reading the Bible. Now, we know that's from Satan! But something happened recently that changed everything for me.

One evening my daughter came into my bedroom, and Lucy looked like she had just struck gold. She was carrying a Bible that was about as big as she is. She was so excited she could barely stand it.

I start reading Psalm 23, and suddenly I'm on Pinterest looking at "How to Paint Your Entryway Stairs in Rustic Fall Colors!"

"Mom, this story is so amazing! It's like, ya know, cray-cray, but awesome! I have to read it to you."

You'd think she was talking about Harry Potter or the latest Pixar movie. But no, she was talking about the story of Joseph in Genesis when his brothers sold him into slavery. Her eyes were wide with excitement.

Now, being the great mom I am, I've always prided myself on how well my kids know their Bible. I think we own 1,242 versions of the Bible for children. But this kid came in my room toting the grown-up NIV.

She said, "Mommy, can I read you some of this story?"

Of course I curled up next to her and listened to the Word of God in the voice of my daughter, read so beautifully and with great expression and enthusiasm. I must say, I wasn't tempted for one minute to check any social media. I was fully engrossed in her reading. Her excitement spilled out in her voice, and I couldn't help but sit up and listen. I was in, hook, line, and sinker.

Honestly, I did get a bit tired after a few stories, and of course she wanted to keep reading way past her bedtime. (Was this kid working me over?) When I finally insisted she go to bed, she excitedly asked me if she could keep the light on so she could keep reading her Bible.

I'd love to tell you I was so inspired I dove headfirst into Leviticus after I put her to bed. I'd love to say I stayed up all night reading until I got to Malachi. But that wouldn't even be close to the truth, and then I'd lose all my credibility with you. So I will confess that instead I watched the *Gilmore Girls* TV reunion: *A Year in the Life*.

So what's the takeaway here?

Should I simply be happy that the next generation in my family is going to be a lover of the Word? Or should I wallow in guilt because my kid is spiritually surpassing me at age nine? Maybe I just need to get back to being like a child. Maybe that's what God wanted me to experience that night: the faith and joy of a child. If so, I'm all in. Right after I check my... Just kidding.

**Maybe that's what God wanted
me to experience that night:
the faith and joy of a child.**

How is your time with God in His Word? Does it feel like a chore, or is it something you truly look forward to? Has God ever spoken to you through a child?

I found this verse, Matthew 19:14, that I thought I'd share: "Jesus said, 'Let the little children come to me.'" He delighted in them because of their purity and who they were, not because of their great accomplishments or what they could do for Him or the kingdom. He delights in us the exact same way. I believe that's how God sees us…as children, pure in heart and mind.

We're the ones who made up all the complicated systems and rules and guidelines on how to draw closer to God. How about we just do it? What if we put down our guidebooks and read *His* book?

I've found it's easier for me to read my Bible consistently if I find a version of the Bible that's easy to understand. Personally, my favorite is the New International Version. I've tried reading *The Message*, but it was a little too far away from the text I grew up with. I've tried the King James Version, but all the fancy pronouns gave me a headache.

One resource I love is the Bible Gateway app for my smart phone, or www.Biblegateway.com; both are free and include audio versions of the Bible. Now I can stream Bible verses any time of day, even while I'm multitasking. And who are we kidding? We're women! When are we *not* multitasking? We probably do to-do lists in our dreams. Also you can get the Bible read to you by James Earl Jones! Who wouldn't want to hear the Bible from Darth Vader?

As a performer I get to be a part of many cool projects. Years ago, I had the opportunity to participate in a celebrity recording of the audio Bible with some really cool Hollywood actors. I like to think that somewhere out there right now someone is listening to Denzel Washington, Blaire Underwood, and me reading Leviticus. (I think the bigger stars got the more exciting chapters. I was assigned the section about boils and curses. But I crushed it!)

This last tip is for all the "Rules Gals" out there. I printed out a plan to read the Bible in one year, and I put it in my Bible. I love the thrill of crossing off verses I've completed. I know it's so third grade, but hey, if it gets me reading, I'm sure God's all good with it. It's actually a personal challenge for me to compete with myself. I want to complete the Bible in less than a year, so this little printout helps keep me on track. And I love crossing off to-do lists. I hope I am setting some good examples for my kids to see their mommy making an effort to connect with God.

I'm going to take this moment to be thankful that God has given me some really great kids. I spend so much of their lives telling them to sit down, stand up, eat, bathe, and repeat. I shout Bible verses at them on the way to school, "'God so looooooved the world!' Say it! Saaaaaay it!" I want them to memorize their verses to pass their tests so they can get into a good college. I need to chill out.

For as long as I can remember, people have been telling me I need to put on the full armor of God daily (Ephesians 6:11-18). But I must admit I never prayed that prayer more than two days in a row. Then I had a stroke of genius: I taught my kids to pray the verses on the way to school. So now every morning we are all suited up to take our stand against the devil's schemes.

I guess having kids has a lot of advantages, including helping parents develop healthy habits. (I barely ever drink soda out of the big bottle anymore or milk out of the carton…at least not if the kids are home.) If I forget to pray the prayer, they are the first ones to remind me!

If they get through school in one piece and have a love for God and His Word, I think they'll be light-years ahead of the game. I can't promise their socks will be matching. If they're wearing socks at all… winning!

Take that, devil!

#motherhoodcrushingit #proverbs32woman

TOP TEN THINGS THAT HAPPEN AS SOON AS YOU DECIDE TO READ YOUR BIBLE

1. A barrage of Facebook alerts come up on your phone. Three new people commented on your dog's new haircut. Now you must like their comments or you will seem rude.

2. While you are scrolling on your phone, your mom calls to chat about the article she's reading in *Prevention Magazine*: "The New Way to Walk Off Belly Fat." She thought you would be interested since you told her you were going to try to lose weight and work out more.

3. When you hang up the phone with your mom, you realize you forgot to take your vitamins. You go into the kitchen, line them up, and google more information about the new supplement you got on Amazon for more focus and energy.

4. While you are taking your vitamins, you remember you forgot to eat breakfast so you decide to fix yourself a bowl of cereal. But then you remember you're out of milk, so you make a grocery list. Then you decide to go through your pantry to see what else you are out of, and you see that leftover Halloween candy you were hiding from your kids. You decide to have just one piece, then just one more.

5. While going through your pantry, you discover how badly you've stacked your plastic containers. You decide you must absolutely take out all the bowls, make sure they have lids, and if not, throw them in recycling.

6. On the way to take out the recycling, you notice the plants haven't been watered, and you find kickballs in your flower bed. You make sure the toys are cleaned out, and you consider if this might be the time to plant sunflowers.

7. On the way back inside, you see how dirty your porch and entryway are, and you notice a spider web. You get out the

broom to sweep the spider web and your porch, and then continue to sweep your entire living room because you haven't done it in ages, and this is the only quiet moment you have to get some light cleaning done, and cleaning is so important!

8. While sweeping, you realize this activity is a cardio workout of sorts, but the steps won't count since you're not wearing your Fitbit. That's when you remember you promised yourself you'd get 10,000 steps on your Fitbit every day, and you were maybe on track until you lost your Fitbit three months ago. You go through all your drawers to find your Fitbit, only to discover the battery is dead. You plug it in and decide to turn on YouTube's "Walk It Off" workout for ten minutes because you want to stay true to your word to yourself.

9. While doing the workout, you realize your phone is dinging because three more people commented on your dog's new haircut. As you lunge for the phone, you trip over your high heels that you forgot to put away after church five days ago. You land hard, and you're pretty sure you sprained your ankle.

10. You gasp and cry out in pain, "Help me, Lord! Please help me!" Then you look over and see your Bible on top of your comfy bed, waiting for you the whole time. You start lamenting over what a bad Christian you are, you ask God to heal your ankle, and you vow to do better tomorrow… right after you check your Instagram. (Your cat got a new bell collar and you want to see if people like it!)

4

FASTING, PRAYING, AND CAPTAIN CRUNCH

Turns out, if you stop eating because you're trying to lose ten pounds, that's not fasting; it's dieting. Fasting has never been a spiritual gift of mine. I've only attempted it a handful of times, and 99 percent of my motivation was desperation. But when my heart is in the right place, when I give things up for Him and not for me, God shows up.

**When my heart is in the right place,
when I give things up for Him
and not for me, God shows up.**

Now, if He were willing to combine this sacrifice with weight loss… well…

I remember a particularly traumatic time many years ago when a family member very close to me was gravely ill. The situation seemed hopeless and frightening, to say the least. I was mad, I was desperate, and I immediately took to drinking water and eating only bread. I didn't know if it was going to help anything, but I had read in the Bible that fasting was used in many circumstances when people wanted to clear their minds and hear from God. I needed to hear God immediately.

I don't know how long that lasted. It may have only been one day, but I remember it not being difficult. I was in such a "face on the floor" phase of my life that food took a clear second to petitioning the throne room of grace to save my loved one's life. I felt as though I'd been lifted out of the trauma of it all, and I had some strange peace. I know I shouldn't call it strange, but it was strange I wasn't completely freaking out!

Long story short, my prayers and the prayers of many others were answered with a big fat healing miracle, and all of our faith was encouraged. Did that happen because I gave up food? I don't know how that factored into the miracle, but I do know I heard God's voice in that time and I was comforted.

A few years later it was time for my church's annual 21-day fast. We were given options of how we wanted to fast: giving up all food, liquid only, doing a Daniel fast, etc. So I decided to design my own program. I gave up all sweets and all drinks except water. Was I desperate for God to move? Not so much. Did I want to lose ten pounds? Desperately! So my motives were not right from day one. And I bet you are not shocked to hear I don't think I lasted one day without cheating.

I don't remember exactly how it ended. Maybe it was a stressful moment at work, and I "accidentally without thinking" ordered a Coke. Maybe I was feeling like a drug addict detoxing in my own house, and I ate my daughter's Rocky Road ice cream and her Captain Crunch Berry cereal right out of the box. (At least I only ate the berries.) Total failure. I called my pastor and told him he needed to preach on fasting because, in Christian words, I "stink at it." He laughed and told me to keep trying.

The next year I was mentally prepared. The 21-day fast (no sugar, no soda, no social media) was going to start on January 1.

I took the kids to the store on New Year's Eve and told them they could get as much sugar as they wanted. We'd have a big night of eating, as long as it was gone by the next morning. I'd been on a binge fest since early December, when the holiday parties ruined all the self-control I had. The kids thought I was the coolest mom ever, and we rang in the New Year with our friends Ben and Jerry and homemade bread by yours truly. Yes, I actually ordered a bread machine for the occasion. This seemed like a logical purchase for a fitting way to end the year. Hey, Jesus loved bread!

I decided this year I was also going to fast from all social media. I knew this might be even harder to give up than sugar, but I was game. This year things seemed different. This time I had a goal in mind. I wanted to hear from God more clearly, and I didn't want anything to stand in the way. Once I began I was shocked to find I actually didn't miss scrolling through recipes and baby photos on social media whatsoever, and I was so happy to have more time to spend with my girls. Lucy decided she was going to join me. She had been learning about fasting, and she chose to give up all sugary treats too. My girl didn't even cheat.

I felt really good for the whole 21 days, and doing it with my daughter was an amazing experience. I'm not saying God came down from heaven and talked to me directly, but I do feel there was some breakthrough, even though I wasn't perfect. God knew my heart and my intentions. I also learned not to be tied to the things of this world. When I was stressed, I couldn't run to the chocolate I keep under my bed (it was eaten, anyway) and I couldn't spend hours scrolling through Instagram. I had to find other ways to cope. Lucy had this brilliant idea that we should fast from TV too, but I had to tell her Mommy hadn't gotten a word from the Lord about that. I still needed my Netflix to fall asleep.

Overall, I'm glad I did it, and I'm not afraid to try it again.

Well, to be honest, all this talk of food is making me hungry.

Have you considered fasting? There are many ways to fast; it doesn't have to be all or nothing. You can choose to fast from a single meal or for a whole day. There are many different plans out there to help guide you.

If you don't want to go the food route, you can give up other things like social media, television, or your smart phone. Even deciding you'll ride in the car without the radio turned on can be a form of fasting as you choose a discipline of silence. Some people unplug one day a week, one weekend a month, and one week out of the year. You can find creative ways to set aside distractions and get your focus in the right place.

In his gospel, Matthew had a few things to say about fasting:

> When you fast, do not look somber as the hypocrites do, for they disfigure their faces so to show others they are fasting...But when you fast, put oil on your head and wash your face, so that it will not be obvious to others that you are fasting, but only to your Father, who is unseen; and your Father, who sees what is done in secret, will reward you (6:16-18).

Keep in mind what Matthew said, and don't post fasting updates on social media. It's not a great idea when people make announcements on Facebook: "I'm doing a fast and I'll be updating everyone daily how it's going with daily selfies in my gym mirror!"

Remember, the enemy knows when we're chasing after God, and that only makes him sharpen his arrows and point them straight at us.

Remember, the enemy knows when we're chasing after God, and that only makes him sharpen his arrows and point them straight at us. He will try to make you think you can't survive, but every time you long for that something you've determined to give up, turn your thoughts to God instead. He will sustain you. He always will.

5

AFRICA WRECKED ME... SORT OF

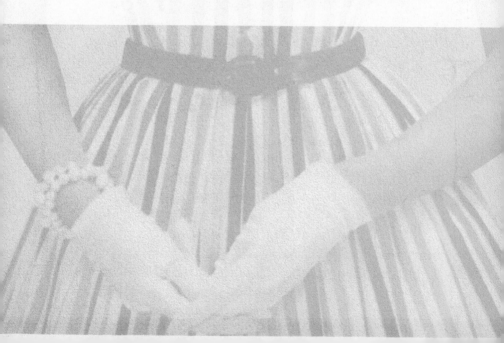

never planned to go to Africa, but I went and it wrecked me…in all the best ways. This was a journal entry I wrote after my first mission trip to South Africa. My first daughter, Lucy, was a year old, and my husband at the time, Ron, and I had come back from this life-changing trip.

I can't sleep. Maybe it's the Prednisone steroid I'm taking to clear up this sinus infection. Or maybe it's the fact that I just spent 14 days in Africa, and I came home reeling. I've been home from Swaziland, South Africa, since Friday. It's now Wednesday at 7:14 a.m. I've been up since 4:00 a.m.

Every single solitary night since I've been home, I wake up in the night. I can't sleep to save my life. I can't stop the hamster wheel that is rolling round and round in my head. My thoughts are all over the place. I remember going through bouts of pregnancy insomnia, and this is fairly reminiscent but far deeper. And I didn't get a kid out of the deal this time!

When I set out to go to Africa, my only hope was to serve

some wonderful kids. But in many ways I think I got way more than I ever could have given.

I was scheduled to do a fund-raiser for a charity founded by Janine Maxwell called Heart for Africa, so I read her autobiography, *It's Not Okay with Me*, and it was life-changing, to say the least. The book told the story of this businesswoman who went to Africa, and she was emotionally and spiritually broken by her experience. She started off going on one mission and then another and another. She was helping orphans find homes. Now she's a full-time minister living in Swaziland.

I was just going to read the book to get some background for the fund-raiser. I had no idea how much it would affect my being. When I wiped myself off the floor after blubbering for three days, I called the author of the tear-stained book. The next thing I knew, I found myself actually talking about going to Africa with Janine. We met for coffee with her husband, Ian.

When she invited me to go, my immediate response was, "No, I can't leave my baby daughter!"

Janine looked me straight in the eye and said, "Really? These kids don't have a mommy."

Did she have to pull out the big guns?

Four months later, I was on the plane to Africa. Don't *ever* tell God where you won't go. You'll end up in a whale! (You do get my Jonah joke, right?)

Don't *ever* tell God where you won't go. You'll end up in a whale!

So I went to Africa. And now I have a confession to make. I think I was happier there. Is that crazy? How can that be?

It all seems like a dream from some far-off distant land that keeps haunting my normal, everyday, crazy, stress-filled life here on Planet Kerri. The haunting isn't a bad thing either. I find myself thinking of my experiences and longing to be back there. I know it's a humanitarian effort, some might say, to do a short-term mission trip like this one. But the longing in my spirit to return is clearly for selfish reasons. I don't want to be selfish, but most of the time I find myself feeling that way. Maybe sometimes I do things just to look good on the outside, knowing it will make a great post on Facebook. What is wrong with me?

I don't know why I'm sad. I love my life and I love my daughter Lucy. I missed her with every fiber of my being when we were away from her. I love the fact that I fly out of bed with both guns blazing to feed her at 6:00 a.m. every morning. I then might get the luxury of bathing alone for ten minutes, a small window to try to have some "quiet time" with God in the shower.

Wait, who am I kidding? That's how it's supposed to be— how I wish it went. But it never goes that way. Maybe it does for Beth Moore.

Here's what it really looks like. Most mornings start with me rushing out of bed and scrambling into the shower, trying to make soapy notes on my arms of my never-ever-ending to-do list that consists of all the duties of a mom, daughter, confidant, friend, counselor, dishwasher/housekeeper, "Elmo play master," touring stand-up comedian, ministry speaker, writer, actor, supermodel wannabe, and Facebook/email addict. (It says in Proverbs 31 that she rose early. Is that because she knew that was the only way she was going to get a hot shower?)

I've been warned and counseled that if I didn't stop this madness in the schedule I was keeping I would one day spontaneously combust. I've come close so many times, but by the grace of God, I'm somehow still standing. There is no other explanation. Right now, as I write this, I feel guilt that I'm not teaching my child Spanish or sign language. Instead, I'm sitting here writing to You, God.

I could have said no to the invitation to Swaziland, since I have enough going on already. I have always been a self-proclaimed diva, through and through. My life song has always sounded something like, "It's all about meeeeeeeeeeeeee!" I was happy to send a check or do a fund-raiser for any great cause, as long as it didn't involve me doing manual labor. Sure, I'd do a "Manicure Mission" (we all go get manicures and read our Bibles) any day! But I have allergies, and that's my sign from God that I'm not meant to be outdoors, unless it's on a patio for lunch. But when I read about the Proverbs 31 woman and all she did, I thought, *That is the example God has for women.* I feel this pressure that we should be living life to the fullest, be intentional with our thoughts, be crazy productive, and—most of all—stay busy.

But when I heard about what was going on with the kids in Africa, and when I saw their pictures, I couldn't say no. These kids were eating dirt, living in the streets, and scouring through garbage cans for scraps. I saw these beautiful faces, and I felt as though they were looking right at me. I didn't want to go, and I was scared out of my mind. Who wants to spend 16 hours on a plane and then five days on a bus to get hot and sweaty? I could just take Bikram yoga if I want to sweat that much.

But I knew I needed to go. In the midst of all my life's craziness, I decided to commit to going to Swaziland, Africa, to spend 14 days helping orphans. I partnered with Janine and

Heart for Africa, a faith-based organization dedicated to helping the children of Africa, especially those with AIDS.

I could write volumes about our experiences there. We saw miracles of healing that you only could read about in books. We did things we never thought we'd do. I even used a contraption called a rake and another one called a Weedwacker. That was comedy material right there. I got a cough after raking, and I convinced everyone I was coming down with malaria.

We were engrossed in helping these truly amazing kids who were celebrating our very presence. I had the pleasure of delivering sandwiches and supplies to a family that hadn't eaten in two days. I can't comprehend the joy they experienced from a simple sandwich, and I was suddenly aware that I can't begin to count how many sandwich crusts I've wasted through my childhood. I'll never ever throw away my crusts again.

I'll never forget when I got to give each of them their very own blanket. Lucy has about 18 blankets—and we live in California where it's warm! (I'm actually not exaggerating. She has 18 blankets. That is nuts!) My baby has an endless supply of blankets, and these kids had none. I became so aware of our abundance and the things we take for granted.

**I became so aware of our abundance
and the things we take for granted.**

In fact, I saw things I take for granted in a whole different light. I met a family of children who are basically raising themselves, literally living a day-to-day existence. They get up, get dressed for school, and walk a long way every day. They don't have a home to do homework in. They live in an abandoned garbage dump. But does that stop them from smiling and dreaming of a better tomorrow? No! They aren't quitters. One boy is even the first in his class. He told me this with pride.

I heard that when they have extra food, they don't hoard it or save it. They go over to their neighbors and share. Their faith is so pure that they know their needs will be met, and they just don't have time to worry about it. I guess life is different when every day is about your basic survival. You'd never know this, though, by the looks on their faces. They showed me what joy looks like. The children smiled and hugged me, and they were so polite and thanked me, but I felt like I should be thanking them for showing me what true innocence and purity look like.

God, do You think I'll ever truly know the simple joys they experience from getting their most basic needs met by the kindness of others? Or am I ruined by what I already have? Is it too late for me? What about my kid?

In Swaziland, people are dying every day from AIDS. A huge population of households are run by children, age six or younger, because their parents have died. They are orphans, left to fend for themselves. In other cases they have a parent, but the father has fled the scene. (And I won't even leave my child alone for five minutes. She might start a fire.)

I visited with one particular family for two days in a row. Amazingly, they are a rare family with both a mom and a dad, and the parents are even together. They have their struggles. They've lost a child, and they have many friends who've died from AIDS. They live with the fear that they themselves could get AIDS, or worse, their children could be sick. Through all the terrible tragedies this couple has gone through, they're still trying to find a way to survive, and from what I've learned, they're both struggling with alcohol, possibly drugs, and prostitution. We smelled marijuana on their property. I find it hard to even imagine what some people are forced to do to survive. But they are parents who are present in their family, and it was a joy to be with those children. We prayed together, and I thanked God for His plans for their lives.

But, God, I have a question. Are You going to restore this family from the life of poverty? I know Heart for Africa has plans to help the dad and mom get real jobs, and the organization has a goal to actually raise $10,000 to build them their very own home. So maybe they could be an example of God's restoration powers. I believe it is possible. Is anything too big for You?

I'm sitting here thinking about this one particular couple, who literally have nothing, yet they still get up every morning and find a way to make it through the day. I remember the look in the mom's eyes, watching me give her children clothes and blankets. Sarah said *thank you* without words. When we prayed, she smiled. There was still a glimmer of hope in her eyes. I have to believe, God, that You are doing something special with her. I've heard she's started to go to church now. I was truly honored she let me into her world, even for a brief moment. She's a much stronger woman than I could ever be.

I pray, God, that You can give me some of her resilience. I pray You could show me how to persevere when I want to throw in the towel. I pray You can show me how to be like a child again, that I can be joyful in the midst of great trials.

I just had this supposedly life-changing experience, and now I'm back in my world with my same problems, and I don't seem to be dealing with them any differently. Why is that? Why didn't Africa make all of my superficial issues and worries go away? Wasn't that what was supposed to happen?

My mind is going nuts right now, and I can't seem to get a handle on my own life. I still freak out over our finances sometimes, and I wonder what sport to put my Lucy in so she can go to college for free. I'm still the same selfish, mixed-up person I was before I went to Africa, but now I've seen too much. I guess I thought I'd come home and be like Mother Teresa or something, that I'd all of a sudden appreciate every single detail of blessing in my life. I thought I'd pray more, listen to more Christian music, and overall be a better woman. The fact that I even have a healthy family should be enough. I just can't seem to be satisfied. I mean, I know I should be able to realize how miraculous You are in my life. I'm just having a tough time right now processing these experiences.

Dear God, if You're reading this right now, please help me. I want to be changed. Please help me not forget what happened to me in Africa. Please help me remember Sarah and her children when I think my life is tough. I look forward to the day I can visit their family again in their new home so I can see just how miraculous You are, God.

Please help me not forget You're still in the miracle business and Your love has no borders. Please help me find a place of peace in the world You've placed me in. Please, God, don't let me slide through this life on earth just barely getting by. I want to go deeper, God. And most importantly, please help me remember I'm not the most important person in the universe.

I love You.

Amen.

Sometimes the stresses of a tragic situation can be so overwhelming that it stops us from doing anything at all. Instead, we say to ourselves, "That mountain is way too big to climb. I'll just sit here at the bottom and eat a sandwich." Well, what if God wants you to go all the way to the top of that mountain because there's someone there who needs a bite of your sandwich? Would you go if you knew someone was there waiting for you to bring her food? Would you trust that He would guide you and protect you the entire way?

Going to Africa was one of the scariest things I've ever done in my whole life. But I can say this with 100 percent certainty: it was a God-ordained journey with a final destination unknown. That adventure is not over, because I can still make a difference right where I am.

As I read that journal entry, I realized I wasn't focusing on all the moments of joy in Africa. But Jesus plainly said we are to take care of widows and orphans, and I had the opportunity to do that in Africa. I could feel good about that. (No, I did not get malaria, by the way!) But I realized God still had work for me to do and decided to start telling people about Heart for Africa to help raise awareness for the plight of those in Africa and for what this organization was doing to help. At my comedy shows I sell the jewelry made by the local women in Swaziland. It's exciting to think I can offer financial help to these amazing people.

**What is God gently talking to you
about that scares you? Where
is God asking you to go?**

So I guess the old saying holds true: "Where there's a prayer, there's a way!" Okay, that's not old. I just made that up. But I like it! Do you?

What is God gently talking to you about that scares you? Where is God asking you to go? If it's outside your comfort zone, it's probably going to be the ride of your life.

Take some time to think about what you might be hearing from God. Is He trying to stretch you? Are you willing to be pliable? Maybe keep a journal to record your thoughts and feelings. This can help you see more clearly what God is asking you to do or what mountain He might want you to climb. Don't worry, He'll be there with you every step of the way!

This verse recently came to my mind: "Peace I leave with you; my peace I give you. I do not give to you as the world gives. Do not let your hearts be troubled and do not be afraid" (John 14:27). I know God spoke those words for Sarah and her children just as much as He spoke them for me and mine.

Speaking of my children, I gotta check on Lucy. She's been way too quiet in the kitchen, and that usually means there's a can of Cheez Whiz involved!

6

IN DEFENSE
OF MARTHA

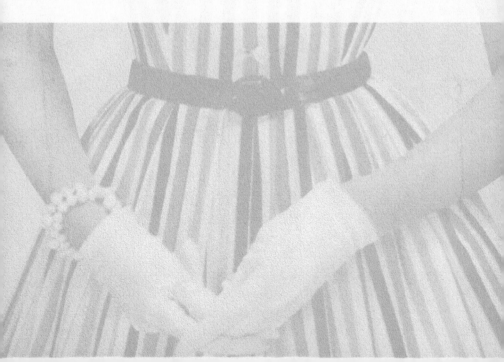

Most of you are probably familiar with the famous Bible story where Jesus visits the home of His friends, Mary, Martha, and Lazarus. Many people have praised Sister Mary (obviously a very holy name), who instead of rushing around with the guests sat at Jesus's feet.

Here is an excerpt from the book of Luke, chapter 10:

> As Jesus and his disciples were on their way, he came to a village where a woman named Martha opened her home to him. She had a sister called Mary, who sat at the Lord's feet listening to what he said. But Martha was distracted by all the preparations that had to be made. She came to him and asked, "Lord, don't you care that my sister has left me to do the work by myself? Tell her to help me!"
>
> "Martha, Martha," the Lord answered, "you are worried and upset about many things, but few things are needed—or indeed only one. Mary has chosen what is better, and it will not be taken away from her" (verses 38-42).

Okay, okay, I get it. Mary was focused on Jesus, her Lord and Savior, and of course giving Him her full attention and devotion was the better choice that day. But I do have one question. If everyone was supposed to be sitting at Jesus's feet, who was supposed to be in charge of the catering? Did they expect Jesus to do the fishes and loaves miracle again? Wouldn't that be kind of rude? Is it so bad that Martha wanted to greet the guests? "Welcome! Snacks are in the kitchen. I've made my special unleavened bread you guys love."

If everyone was supposed to be sitting at Jesus's feet, who was supposed to be in charge of the catering?

Couldn't Martha's love language possibly have been acts of service? (If you aren't familiar with the love language thing, check out *The 5 Love Languages* by Gary Chapman. It's really eye-opening.) Was it so bad that Martha probably stayed up all night the night before the party, cleaning and sweeping her home, working her little tail off, preparing a feast fit for a king? Because, well, the King of the world was coming over.

Everyone has always concentrated on the calm and quiet faith of Mary. "Be a Mary," the world tells us. Even though we live in a Martha world, we are told we are called to "be like Mary" and sit at Jesus's feet. Are they wrong? Probably not. Okay, definitely not.

But what if I was created with more of a Martha disposition? Is that so bad?

I know I'm a Martha. I get where she was coming from. Never in my wildest dreams would I have had all those people over without having several trays of snacks and refreshments ready to hand out. I'm sure

I would scour Pinterest for fabulous ideas, though I probably wouldn't use any of them. I'm never going to be that woman who makes seasonal desserts, like a cake in the shape of the American flag. Sure, I'll eat that cake with wild abandon; I'm just not making it. I would, however, make my old standby: mozzarella caprese on a stick. It's a crowd-pleaser. Or my deviled eggs, but I'm not sure Jesus would like that snack title.

It's ironic that I vowed I'd write this chapter today knowing I was going to a barbecue with some friends later. I had the best intentions of making something fabulous, but in keeping with the tradition of my mother, I plan on going to the grocery store deli and purchasing the potato salad because I saw it's on sale. I will put it in my own Tupperware, I will sprinkle paprika on it, and I will call it homemade. My mother is a champion at church potlucks. Not only does she buy the grocery store's fried chicken, and not only does she put it in her own Tupperware, she adds paper towels to make it appear as though the grease is hers. My grandmother is probably rolling over in her grave right now, feeling all the shame.

Okay, back to Martha. I think she's gotten a bad rap. The desire of Mary's heart was to sit at the feet of Jesus and anoint Him with oil, and that's an awesome thing to want to do for the Lord. But who do you think swept the floor everyone was sitting on? Who do you think made sure Jesus had a nice snack after His journey? Martha! Yes—Martha, Martha, Martha!

I guess I have a lot to learn about what Jesus was really wanting in that moment. I know I need to learn about trying to have more of a "Mary heart" when it comes to intimacy with Jesus. But I am curious if the Proverbs 31 Woman was more like Martha or Mary. On the one hand she got quite a lot done in one day and she did have three jobs. On the other hand it *clearly* states she had servants. No, not just a maid, not just a nanny, servants…*plural*! So we know this woman at least knew how to delegate.

I know we all make choices about how we spend our time. And joking aside, if Jesus were coming to my house, I think I might be a combination of both of these sisters. I might freak out and make sure my home was spotless, but I'm also pretty sure the moment Jesus walked in my door, I'd be some sort of fan girl, probably literally grabbing Him by the ankles and yelling, "I'm sorry for all the times I ignored You! Please forgive me! Bless me, oh Lord. I'm not worthy! I'm not worthy!"

I mean, let's think about it. Mary and Martha really did both take in the significance that Jesus, the Savior of all mankind, the Creator of the universe, wanted to be their friend and hang out with them. It's huge! It's epic! I have celebrity friends, but Jesus's star power is on a whole other level.

As I sit here writing and pondering the situation as it could apply to me, I see the perspectives of both sisters. Martha loved Jesus so much that she wanted everything to be perfect for His visit. She was willing to work her fingers to the bone and do whatever it took to make her home lovely, to make the food appetizing, and to make her guests feel loved and welcome.

Martha loved Jesus so much that she wanted everything to be perfect for His visit.

I'm guessing Martha was also similar to those of us who are approval junkies. She was hoping Jesus might comment on her decorating or those delicious honey-filled matza turnovers. Maybe she was hoping God would say, "Well done, my good and faithful Martha. You crushed this party! I am so proud of you." When she approached Jesus, I don't think she was trying to get her sister into trouble. I think she wanted to get Jesus's attention. I imagine she was struggling with the ever-popular fairness doctrine. She didn't think it was fair that she was doing all the work. Mary was also listed as co-hostess on the invite, but Martha didn't think she was carrying her load. I see her point, don't you?

I know I'm taking liberties with the story, because the Bible doesn't give us many details. For centuries we've been told we need to be more like Mary and stop being such Marthas, but I wanted to try to see things from Martha's perspective. I think she loved Jesus so much she was willing to do whatever it took to make His time in her home perfect. But I also understand that in doing that, she forgot the fact that all Jesus really longed for was her company. On the other hand, without Martha the guests would have been starving.

So was Martha's heart in the right place? Sure. Was she maybe trying to show off a little bit with her culinary and homemaking skills? Probably. I believe she was well-intentioned in wanting her Savior's attention, but she went a little overboard in the preparation and forgot about having actual intimacy with Jesus. Now Mary, on the other hand, took the more direct route. She was not complicated. She simply wanted to spend time with Jesus, and that's exactly what she did. I suppose she wasn't the multitasker in the family because Martha took care of all that. Mary loved Jesus and was probably pondering the fact that their time with Him was short. She seemed to have an empathetic heart. In a lot of situations taking the simple approach is a great decision. But women like me seem to overthink things a lot of the time, just like Martha

We've all done that, right? I can think of many church functions and prayer meetings I have prepared for and hosted in my home, and I spent the entire time making sure people had enough drinks and snacks instead of participating in anything even looking like prayer. I was too busy being Martha. I own it.

If I met Martha today, I'd say, "Girl, I ain't mad at ya! You do you! Just remember Jesus doesn't love you for your snacks and clean threshing floor. He loves you because He loves you. End of story. And every moment you can spend with Him is precious."

I believe this principle can also be applied to the other people in our life. Are you the type of person who gets so excited about all the planning and production for a family reunion or a gathering of friends that you miss the entire point of the get-together in the first place? Ask yourself this question: If a bunch of loved ones are sitting at the table talking after a meal, are you capable of enjoying their company and *not* jumping up to clear the dishes? Have you ever caught yourself cleaning and sweeping up in the middle of a party when (a) the party isn't over, or (b) it's not your house?

Okay, to be honest I'm guilty of all of that and more. I've hosted countless gatherings in my house where I spent 90 percent of my time in my kitchen. And then I discovered paper plates. I mean, really cute paper plates, not just the ugly white ones. I'm telling you, paper plates have changed my life. I used to always feel obligated to serve my guests on my grandmother's fancy dishes, or at least the "good plates," as my mom would call them. After all, I was raised by the consummate Southern "hostess with the mostess."

Not to out my mother, but we still aren't even allowed into certain rooms of her house unless company is over. Did any of you have that kind of mom? You know, the one with the plastic covers on the furniture in the living room that nobody—and I mean *nobody*—ever sat in? I bet Martha had plastic furniture covers for sure!

But back to my paper plate story. When I started serving guests food on my cute paper plates at my parties, I discovered this freed up hours of my time. I loved it so much that now I serve my kids food on paper plates *every* day! Yes, they eat their meat loaf off of emoji dinnerware, and they think I'm a cool mom. And I'm saving money and water by not running the dishwasher. So I guess you could say I'm sort of an environmentalist hero of sorts.

I know we can learn a lot from the stories of Mary and Martha. They both were true worshipers, each in her own way. We don't have to be a Mary or a Martha. Both sisters had redeeming qualities God wanted to highlight. Let's not focus on all of Martha's faults and how perfect her sister was. We all know no one is perfect. But we also need to take a look at our own relationship with Jesus and see which side we fall on. Are we more concerned with the preparation of being with Jesus or the actual intimacy He longs to have with us?

**Are we more concerned with
the preparation of being with
Jesus or the actual intimacy
He longs to have with us?**

Where do you think you fall on the Mary/Martha spectrum?

In our spiritual walk with God, we're going to fulfill different roles at different times. Every church needs someone who can make an epic strawberry cake or deviled eggs. But make sure your priorities are in the right place so you don't miss the main event, and that is communing with the One who gives you true peace of mind: Jesus Christ.

Take some time when you are alone, and ask God to show you any areas where you are a little off balance. Listen to what you hear, and look for ways to correct what God is revealing to you.

Maybe the next time you're invited to host an event or to participate in something that would usually bring you great stress with all the preparations, find an easier way to do it. God invented catering for a reason. Don't miss the moment!

That reminds me, I've got to run to the store now and get my "homemade" potato salad and put it in my own bowl!

P.S. The Dollar Store has the cutest paper plates! Check 'em out!

P.P.S. If you are one of those Pinterest chicks who makes the most perfect appetizers and desserts from scratch, please find me on Facebook or Twitter. I want to be friends with you! I'm hungry.

KERRI'S FAMOUS CAPRESE
ON A STICK RECIPE

Ingredients

1 cup balsamic vinegar
Cherry or grape tomatoes
Mini mozzarella cheese balls
    (or one regular-size ball cut into bite-size pieces)
Fresh basil leaves
Toothpicks
Salt and black pepper

Directions

Bring balsamic vinegar to a boil in a saucepan over high heat, then lower heat to medium and simmer until it's the consistency of very thin maple syrup, about 10 minutes. Pour into a bowl and let cool.

Cut tomatoes in half. Thread a mini mozzarella cheese ball, basil leaf (fold in half if large), and a tomato half onto a toothpick. Repeat with remaining ingredients. Sprinkle with salt and pepper, then drizzle with cooled balsamic reduction.

KERRI'S FAMOUS CRACK
CHICKEN IN THE CROCK-POT
(Great for potlucks or to take if
someone has a baby or dies)

Ingredients
4 chicken breasts
16 ounces cream cheese
1 dry packet Hidden Valley Original Ranch Salad
    Dressing & Seasoning Mix
Hot sauce to taste

Directions
Place all ingredients in a slow cooker. Cook on low setting for 6 to 8 hours, or on high for 4 to 6 hours, until chicken is cooked through.

Uncover. Shred the chicken and mix all ingredients until incorporated.

You can serve this on buns like a sandwich, by itself, or over rice.

You can add a little hot sauce to taste.

Note: I like to add carrots and celery to the slow cooker to make me feel like I made something healthy.

7

ONE IS THE LONELIEST NUMBER

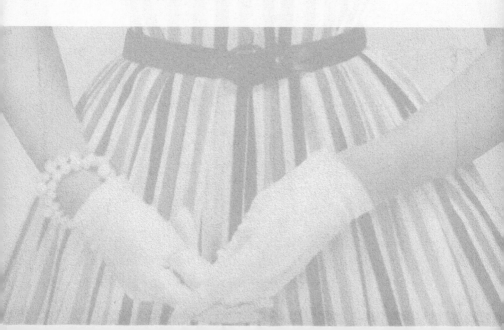

'm usually the one hosting parties and planning girls' nights, and you'll often find me in the middle of a lot of group activities. So if you met me, you might not guess that I was a lonely kid. I can clearly remember desperately struggling, even when I was very young, with the fear of being alone. It didn't help that I went to a Christian school with 90 kids total, kindergarten through eighth grade. My kindergarten started with only four or five girls, and by the time I hit third grade, I guess I had weeded most of them out. By fifth grade, I was the sole surviving female in my class. I attended a Dutch Reformed denomination, and I was an Italian Catholic, so I didn't exactly blend either.

Yes, I have some amazing dodgeball and soccer skills, because my only playmates were boys. Recess was a time of true terror for me. I literally freaked out every day, worried that no one would want to play with me. I know that's hard for you to believe, my trusted reader, because you must be imagining how adorable and funny I was, right? Let's just say you don't become a stand-up comedian because you had a normal childhood.

In seventh grade the heavens parted and God sent me Jennie Sollars. We were the only two girls in the entire grade, and she saved me that year. We shared lunches, we sang songs like "Stand by Me" at the top of our lungs as we walked home from school, and we bonded over the cute boys she knew from public school (also known as the Devil's Playground). I was beyond ecstatic to have a BFF. We got matching lockets with bears on them in real gold plating. I still have mine. We also both decided to get bangs...spiked bangs, and we gave each other haircuts in my mother's bathroom. You should have seen the look on my mother's face when she saw our new 'dos!

Let's just say you don't become a stand-up comedian because you had a normal childhood.

The next year we both moved to other towns, but we vowed to stay in touch and be BFFs forever. We spent hours chatting on the phone. The phone was my favorite thing in my whole house. I remember when I had to drag the cord into another room and lie on the floor to get some privacy while my little brother listened in on the other side of the door. Or if he was really stealthy he could listen in on the other phone by pressing the mute button. I'm sure he learned that from my mother.

In high school and college, I did whatever was necessary to sit at the right lunch table, join the right sororities and clubs, and of course date the right guys. I never wanted to be alone on a Friday night—or on Saturday, for that matter—and the right social calendar was key. I had a boyfriend in high school for two years who was on the football team. My dad wanted to get him a shirt that said, "I may not be very smart but I can lift heavy objects!" But hey! I looked good in that letterman's jacket.

In college at the University of Michigan, I was a musical theater major, and productions were satisfying for me because I felt a sense of belonging in every show. I loved the nomadic lifestyle, jumping from show to show, and eventually I moved out here to La La Land with a couple friends and no money so I could pursue my dream of acting.

It was terrifying. I remember the day my mom and dad were leaving me to go back to Georgia after moving me into my new apartment in LA. When my mom hugged me, she said, "There are *no* Christians in California. But if you end up in a church with Tom Cruise, tell him I said hello."

My dad handed me a handwritten map he had drawn with magic marker to help me navigate the mean streets of LA. Yes, this was before GPS. Can you imagine? We had to get around without Google Maps? Yes, kids, it was the wild, wild west.

I so clearly remember standing all by myself in the cold, dark hallway of the Oak Wood apartments in Marina Del Rey, watching my mom and dad walk back to the minivan. Tears were streaming down my face. I felt totally alone. In that instant I was questioning my decision to move out to Los Angeles, or "Sodom and Gomorrah" as my mother called it, to pursue a life in show business. What was I thinking? I didn't have any connections, and all I had to fall back on was a degree in musical theater.

I quickly started working three jobs (yes, all at one time), going on auditions, and as my boyfriend Patrick Swayze would say, "having the time of my life!" That was many years ago. I stayed here in Tinseltown, got married, had two kids, got divorced, and recently started a serious relationship with Netflix and the Hallmark Channel. I cheat on them with Amazon Prime occasionally.

My mom loves the movie *Steel Magnolias* with Sally Field and Julia Roberts. The women in this movie bonded for life as they all gathered at Dolly Parton's beauty shop. I want a Dolly Parton in my life. (Not that I want her to do my hair.) When I go to a local coffee shop or hair salon, I don't even see anyone having a conversation. Laptops, iPads, and cell phones are demanding everyone's full attention. Now, in LA's defense, I've actually found out this problem is not unique to this city. Women from all over the country have expressed the same type of struggles to me, even though their lives might appear fulfilling and busy (at least on the Internet they do). I hear women all the time say they are lonelier than they ever have been and feel isolated in a sea of "digital connections."

I know a million people, and I would venture to say a million people know me. Many, many people call me their friend. But I want real friends. I want people to "do life with," not share Instagram comments with heart emojis. Have my relationships really been relegated to expressing ourselves with "applause" emojis and photos with bunny ears? #snapchat

Maybe I watched too many episodes of *Friends* and *How I Met Your Mother*. Maybe it's a fantasy to find an age-appropriate yet diverse group of like-minded friends that meet at the old watering hole/coffee shop/pub to discuss life's problems and share advice and laughter.

Where are those people? Where is my Ross or Monica?

They say (whoever *they* are) that you have to be intentional about cultivating community. Was it like that when we were kids? Remember when we just walked up to the kids jumping rope, got in line, and jumped? Do you think men have this problem making friends? They just show up on a basketball court, see a bunch of sweaty, grunting men playing, and yell, "I go next!" They don't even need to talk. They just run up and down a court together, they say a few congratulatory words to whoever wins, and then walk away satisfied. I need more than that. Also, I hate sweating.

Holidays tend to be the worst. Last Easter I decided not to go home to visit my parents in Georgia, and instead I chose to stay here in town. I got my girls up early, took them to church in their new dresses, and dropped them off in Sunday school. As I took my place in the service, I looked around and saw all the happy families sitting together. I saw well-dressed husbands lovingly draping their arms around their wives. And then I had the cold, hard realization that I was totally and utterly alone.

How did I end up here with that same sinking feeling I had when I was nine years old, back when I feared no one would play with me at recess? Now I had no one to play with on Easter. No one was going to give me those scrumptious chocolate Cadbury eggs. There were no brunch reservations with friends, and no one was waiting for me with a home-cooked feast.

How did I end up here with that same sinking feeling I had when I was nine years old, back when I feared no one would play with me at recess?

After church on this glorious Easter day, I had nowhere to go. It hurt right in my gut. I love my church, but it's big. It's not easy to find a "tribe." I couldn't attend the couples' small group anymore, I was too old (by a long shot) for young adults ministry, and most of the women in the other small groups were at least 15 years my senior.

So there I was, in my pastel pink dress and hat, with my two incredibly dressed girls, heading home to my empty house on that beautiful sunny Easter afternoon. Before I got married, I had a million single friends I could gather together for a holiday celebration at a moment's notice. We'd even jaunt off to Mexico if we felt like it. But now it seemed everyone had settled into their nuclear families, and I didn't want to intrude on their time by inviting myself over.

When I was married, the four of us felt like a complete family celebration. I had someone to partner with, someone to co-parent with, someone who would light up the grill or at least watch one kid while the other one ran to the buffet line to get more cheese cubes and soft serve ice cream for $25.99. On this morning I had no desire to go out by myself with the minions, play referee, and stare at the swarms of families posing for photos and gorging on too much ham. When we got home I quietly put on some sweatpants and let the kids play outside.

That afternoon a friend sent me a message: "Let me ask my husband if you guys can join us for dinner." It was sweet, but her text made me feel even more like a loser, like my girls and I had to be approved to join in someone else's holiday.

Then I got a little irritated with myself. Couldn't I just be happy with my two kids and find some fulfilling activity to do? After all, wasn't I being a bit selfish? This day was about the miracle of Jesus. He died for my sins and conquered death, and here I was, having a pity party.

I wondered what God was thinking. Was He looking down on me, annoyed, saying, "Snap out of it! I sent you My Son! Be happy!" No, that's not my God. I think He was looking down from heaven understanding the loneliness I was feeling. He experienced the very same thing many times when He walked this earth. I believe that's one of the reasons God made Himself into one of us, so He could know all the joys and sorrows of the human condition. And so He could go to that cross to give us eternal life and spare us from judgment. But also with that came the promise that we don't have to struggle through this life alone.

Jesus knew what it was like to be deserted. His very own crew left Him in the Garden of Gethsemane.

> Then Jesus went with his disciples to a place called Gethsemane, and he said to them, "Sit here while I go over there and pray." He took Peter and the two sons of Zebedee along with him, and he began to be sorrowful and troubled. Then he said to them, "My soul is overwhelmed with sorrow to the point of death. Stay here and keep watch with me."
>
> Going a little farther, he fell with his face to the ground and prayed, "My Father, if it is possible, may this cup be taken from me. Yet not as I will, but as you will."
>
> Then he returned to his disciples and found them sleeping. "Couldn't you men keep watch with me for one hour?" he asked Peter (Matthew 26:36-40).

I mean, He told His best friends, "I'm overwhelmed with sorrow to the point of death," and they still didn't do anything for Him. They just fell asleep. They didn't even try to comfort Him. Less than a few hours later, one of His disciples sold Him for a few measly dollars, and then Peter pretended he never even knew Him! That is intense. In comparison, not having anyone to go to brunch with isn't so bad. But there I go comparing again. It's not like my small first-world problems matter any less to God. If one of my kids stubs her toe and I can barely see a mark, I will still scoop her up into my arms to comfort her. I'm there to help take away the hurt in any way I can.

I had to lean into God's comfort that Easter, and my day did get better when we were invited to our neighbors' impromptu barbecue. It was just the three of us with Larry and Bronwyn and their three boys. I sat blissfully enjoying delicious food cooked on one of those round grill tops drinking lemonade with the biggest smile on my face you could imagine. They have no idea what that last-minute invitation meant to me. It's as though God told them to invite us. Actually, I know He did. I know God cares about our smallest needs; each and every one is important to Him. He knew my heart was aching to feel I belonged somewhere. He felt my sadness, and He sent me some angels right on my block.

These past months I made a vow to make more of an effort to find my community. My friend Susie invited me to a local ladies Bible study, and I'm really enjoying it. We text each other between meetings with prayer requests and praise reports. I met so many great women in that group, so I started some casual prayer nights in my house when I'm home on a Saturday. I open my house and invite my friends to come and pray. It's not formal. We listen to worship songs on YouTube, and the kids play in the playroom and sometimes even join in. I'm passionate about prayer, so why not find others who share that passion? It's been a great way to bond with new women in my life, and I slowly feel as if I'm making some lasting connections. And we're doing my favorite activities: praying, worshiping, and seeking God. (And the best part is we're usually in bed by 11:00 p.m.!)

I'm passionate about prayer, so why not find others who share that passion?

This month was Mother's Day. For the first time in ages I wasn't traveling on a comedy tour. Instead of lamenting because I was alone, I was more proactive. I told my ten-year-old, Lucy, we were going to plan a fun day together. I picked my favorite place to eat brunch, and then I chose my favorite bakery to get cakes. (Have you tried Nothing Bundt Cakes? You'll thank me if you go. They are the best I've ever tasted.) My daughters surprised me with breakfast in bed, which consisted of three chocolate chip cookies, a glass of milk, and an egg. That was marvelous.

We went to church and then to brunch, and I invited our good friend to join us. Lucy picked a holiday-appropriate movie for us to enjoy in honor of Mother's Day: *Throw Momma from the Train*. It was one of my favorite holidays of all time. My friend had taken them shopping and they bought me a red strapless jump suit they presented to me that night. Normally I would not have the self-confidence to wear this type of JLo style. But since it was from my kids, Mommy rocked the jumpsuit!

I guess it does take a little effort to fight off the loneliness we all can battle from time to time. God wanted me to look around and see what He's given me, and He wanted me to know I am truly loved. Sometimes community and family come in all different shapes and sizes. It's up to us to recognize the important people God placed in our lives and be grateful.

Are you feeling lonely? Do you have a spouse who never makes you feel appreciated on special occasions? What can you do to avoid the disappointment? My friend, who is a single mom, says her sons almost always forget Mother's Day and her birthday. This year she bought her own concert tickets and planned the whole day herself. Her proactive approach really worked, and she got to do what she wanted this year without the disappointment of unmet expectations.

Sometimes community and family come in all different shapes and sizes. It's up to us to recognize it and be grateful.

When are the times you feel the loneliest? What can you do to change your circumstances? Have you considered joining a Bible study or a group that would give you some new connections? Even if your church isn't offering something, you can easily look at other churches or women's groups in your community to see if something fits your desires and schedule.

In those times of loneliness, listen for the lies the enemy might be telling you about yourself. If you are hearing anything negative, ask yourself, "Is that really how God would talk about me? Is that really the truth?" Take a moment to pray and ask God to reveal the truth about your situation. Find a verse in the Bible that you feel describes how God really feels about you and how much He loves you. Put it on a sticky note on your bathroom mirror. My house is filled with sticky notes. I need a lot of reminding.

And of course in addition to all of this…there is always Netflix! Netflix got me through some tough times, and I don't have to share my remote! God is good!

8

I'M FAILING
FIRST GRADE

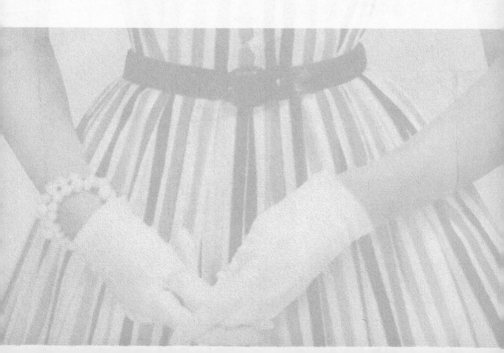

'm failing first grade. No, I'm not kidding. I'm failing first grade. I never thought I would turn into one of *those* moms. You know, the ones who believe raising a high achiever starts with the kind of music you play over your belly when you're pregnant. I've seen those moms. Remember, I live in LA. They are everywhere.

I have a neighbor who literally sent her child to a preschool where the chef was from the Cordon Bleu Institute. She said he was in class with Steven Spielberg's kids, and she told me to my face she already knew which Ivy League college her son would be attending. Mind you, her son happened to be eating the grass behind her as she spoke. I secretly congratulated myself on being the cool mom who didn't care that my child's idea of entertainment was to put a bucket over her head and run into walls. (Have you've seen *Parenthood*? I knew that would be my kid someday.)

My daughters are happy and healthy and, might I add, funny. (They are the children of two comedians, so they didn't have a choice.) But I have to confess something: I like to win. I'm competitive to a fault, and I got that from my own mother. My family is so competitive that board games have basically been outlawed in my home for fear the neighbors will call the cops because we are being too loud…again!

After I had my first child, I'd look at all the fancy moms who made organic baby food and breastfed their kids until puberty because of the DHA or whatever vitamin they say it provided with a mocking eye. That in itself was a form of arrogance. I just knew deep down my kid was better than theirs. I mean, I had proof. Lucy was born at 10.6 pounds. She was so fat she looked like a pig you would see roasting at a luau. Right there from the get-go, I was #motherhoodcrushingit.

> **I secretly congratulated myself on being the cool mom who didn't care that my child's idea of entertainment was to put a bucket over her head and run into walls.**

I sleep-trained her, and I sat smugly in baby class listening to other moms lament about sleepless nights. She walked at nine months, and it seemed like she talked at nine days. I never had any issues with her, and I found a sense of pride in that. She came on stage with me at my shows, and she wowed the audience with her charm. Everything she did was perfection, and I have the grandparents to back up this story. I actually used to plant her in my audience, and when she started crying, I would make a big fuss, asking who would bring a toddler to a comedy show. I would mortify my audience with my rudeness. Then my parents would bring Lucy on stage, and she would immediately do something adorably planned and call me mom. It was magic, I tell you!

So all was good in motherhood…until my perfect baby turned into a toddler. She was two going on thirty, and she let it be known that she was the keeper of all the knowledge in all the world. She was never wrong.

We called her "Loophole Lucy." One time while she was potty training, we saw her pour water into the child potty. Then she said, "Look, Mommy! I go pee-pee. Can I have my candy now?"

Once she was jumping on a trampoline, and she had an accident in her pants. When questioned, she said, "No, Daddy, a big rain cloud came, and it hit me in the butt!" Did I mention I know she'll make a great lawyer someday?

I told Lucy, "I'm going to have a kid who actually likes me!" After raising my little alpha dog firstborn, a leader who was going to end up either in jail or running a country, I thought God would bless me with a sweet, docile child with a quiet smile and an agreeable spirit. I just forgot one important fact: this second child would also be the product of two comedians, and she too would share my genes.

When the second child popped onto the scene, I had no idea what was in store for us. There is nothing docile in any of her DNA. Ruby has never been one to take a back seat to anyone, including her sister. She was born with impeccable timing and can steal anyone's show with the right dance moves, a photogenic pose, or a perfect smile. She has all of her sister's energy, pizzazz, and more. Teachers called her "active and kinetic." (This means "your kid is disrupting my class and breaking things, but I'm not allowed to say that so bluntly.")

My girls are exactly three years apart, so Lucy has taken the lead in life's milestones. She's met all of them with ease and usually early. Sometimes her drive in school scares me, like the time she got an A- on a test—and was mad about it. Then she wanted me to order her a math book for summer reading. I was looking at her bewildered, thinking, *Who are you? I mean, I know you're smart. But who are you getting this brain from?* I got a C in math and my parents threw me a party. This kid was complaining about an A-? (Note to self: Hide all my report cards. Actually, just burn them.) Well, at least she might go to college for free, so that's comforting.

Ruby, however, has sailed through preschool and kindergarten mostly on her charm. She's more like her mother. Her kindergarten teacher said, "If I could teach Ruby for the rest of my life, I would be satisfied!" Yes, I'll take all the credit for that, Mrs. G!

Because of her stellar ability to enchant everyone she meets, I was in no way prepared for the email I got this year, on Ruby's *first* day in first grade.

> Hello, Ms. Pomarolli,
>
> We caught Ruby in the boys' bathroom today, up on top of the stalls. We also would request she not wear her cowboy boots to school, as she is quite adventurous on the monkey bars.

Or the letter we got on the second week of first grade:

> Dear Ms. Pomarolli,
>
> Ruby was lifting her shirt up in front of other students today in line. Please reinforce proper boundaries at home.

Or my favorite:

> Dear Ms. Pomarolli,
>
> Today Ruby gave one of the other children a "thumbs-down" sign. Please talk to her about peaceful communication at home.
>
> P.S. A rumor is going around that she stabbed another student with a pencil, but it has not been confirmed.

I read these notes, and I thought, *Good grief, I gave birth to a brawler.* I wanted to write the teacher and say:

Dear Mrs. Bell,

I'm sorry Ruby was in the boys' bathroom, but that's not entirely her fault; we shop at Target. Do you remember the 2017 Target Bathroom War? They made all bathrooms a "safe zone," and if you were any gender you could use the bathroom you felt comfortable with. That means dudes were in the women's bathrooms!

And seriously, my kid is getting written up for doing a "thumbs-down" sign? Are you kidding? Do you know what we used to do to each other with a dodgeball in the 1980s and '90s? Come on! I say she's innocent if it doesn't leave a mark!

Respectfully,
Ruby's Mom

Ruby did not take to first grade at all. She kept putting on her backpack and trying to go back to kindergarten. And can I be totally candid? I don't blame her. Her kindergarten teacher, Mrs. Grey, had nap times and cookies. Her first-grade teacher has a very no-nonsense style of teaching, and it works for a lot of children. I'm just used to teachers who are a bit more relaxed. I tried to make a delightful joke once and she just stared at me blankly. I knew we were in for a long year.

In all honesty, these instances and the low marks on her first report card actually brought out some serious emotions in me. I didn't even know they were there. I realize children are not born to be pawns in our game of telling the world we're superior. And I am completely aware of the fact that giving first-graders letter grades is insane. But I drank the private school Kool-Aid, and I put her in this school full of teachers who love Jesus, so I have to play by their rules.

At a parent-teacher conference at the beginning of the year, Ruby's grades were all less than stellar…except for lunch! I didn't even know how to react. Do I punish a six-year-old for failing a history test that

I couldn't have passed myself? What happened to A-B-C and 1-2-3? These kids were reading stories and doing fractions.

On the wall in the hallway, I saw Ruby's essay about who she would like to meet the most in the whole world. She wrote, "I would like to meet Donald Trump and go to Chick-fil-A with him because he is a gorgeous man." The teacher wanted me to know she did not learn that in class. I just took my Republican views and silently slipped away.

Later in the semester, Ruby had to write a story and dictate it to her parents. We were supposed to write down what she said, word for word, and not edit. Her story read, "Prince the singer came to Ruby's eighteenth birthday party. They had cake, and then there was purple rain. Prince went in the water with the boys and everyone sang." How could that not be an A+? I mean, come on. The creativity! Yes, my kids listen to '80s music, and they might think Bon Jovi was a Christian band. "Livin' on a Prayer" and "Lay Your Hands on Me!" They love the good stuff. What can I tell ya?

I don't think Ruby was a favorite this year, and why am I not okay with that?

As I sit here awaiting the end of the school year, I'm confused and sort of perplexed at myself for letting all this stuff get to me. I don't think Ruby was a favorite this year, and why am I not okay with that? Why am I freaking out over the fact that she spelled *finally* and *Tuesday* wrong? Her handwriting is a hot mess, and I've almost had aneurisms trying to get her to sit down and write sentences. Don't get me started on those evil dioramas and science projects. I can't take it anymore. You really think a first-grader is going to make an airplane from popsicle sticks and string? These kinds of assignments just stress out parents, forcing us to remember how bad we were at these projects in the first place. All I do is scream spelling words and Bible verses at her all week in preparation for tests on Fridays. I'm sick of tests and flash cards and progress reports and tutors and speech therapy after school. It's all too much.

I never knew it was going to be this hard. I wasn't prepared.

It's almost June, and I want to pull out what's left of my hair. I've stopped caring about what I pack in school lunches. I think I put some leftover crème brûlée and a hunk of fake cheese and some chips in somebody's lunchbox last week. I called it "dessert nachos."

I've tried to connect with Ruby's teacher and not let her words hurt me. There have been more emails and passive-aggressive comments than I care to mention. (Not just by me!) I get it. She's not a fan of my kid, and there's not much I can do about it. And if there were, should I? I've felt at times my child was being segregated in the class because she's not learning as fast as the others. I've read between the lines in emails from her teacher that Ruby might not be, shall we say, the joy to teach that she was last year. Or maybe I'm just oversensitive.

What did I do wrong? She was breastfed. She doesn't drink soda (all that often). How much brainwashing can I do between gymnastics, ballet, trying to feed her, bathing her (on Wednesdays), and trying to instill these godly values I know are so important?

Her talent show is this week, and we've been rehearsing a poem she wanted to recite. It's one we say every night before bed. It was either that or her Tina Turner solo. Hey, she already had the costume! We put some of her favorite scriptures together, and we made it into a poem. We called it our "Declarations."

So the talent show was last night. Guess who was the MC? Yes, it's always a joy to do comedy and emcee for grade schoolers who don't think I'm that funny. My daughter Lucy sang "Gravity" from the Broadway show *Wicked*, and yes, she brought down the house. Don't believe me? Ask Facebook. Umm…her video tore it up! Yes, I'm Mama Rose. Sue me. It was amazing.

Later it was time for Ruby to take the stage. I gave her the mic, and I whispered ever so sweetly, "Don't screw up!"

That little whippersnapper grabbed the mic like a pro. She said, "My name is Ruby McGehee. I'm in first grade, and this is a poem about how God feels about me and you too. Hope you enjoy it." She then recited the words I had taught her since she was little.

You see, when Ruby was born the doctors told me there was a lot wrong with her little body and mind. She was diagnosed with several issues, including low muscle tone. They predicted she might need physical therapy, and if it didn't get better, she would need leg braces or a walker. She was in the NICU for a long time, hooked up to tubes and wires and oxygen. Doctors told me she had complications with her brain and chromosomes, and they used the word *incurable*.

I remember hearing those diagnoses and feeling as though I were being stabbed in the heart. Nothing can prepare you for the news that your child is going to be mentally and possibly physically disabled. I had been a woman of faith, and I had witnessed healing miracles for years. But the doctors were talking about my child, and I didn't even know how to breathe, much less pray. As I recovered from my C-section and tried to process all we were learning about our little girl, I took life one hour at a time.

My friends and family came to the hospital to give prayers and encouragement. My friends from my church even called me one night to say they were praying and God had led them to Psalm 103: "[God] heals all your diseases." They reminded me that as Christians we have the right to ask God to heal anything and everything, and we can expect good results.

As Christians we have the right to ask God to heal anything and everything, and we can expect good results.

I knew this to be true…for other people. I knew Jesus healed… other people. I knew miracles happened…for other people. But could it or would it happen for my baby? Or were the doctors right when they said very clearly, "Your child will never dance like the other kids or go to regular school like the other kids. She will never last 15 minutes in a regular classroom. She will have severe delays in a lot of areas, including learning and speech."

But God said, "With Me, all things are possible." Who was I going to believe?

The doctors gave me handbooks on her diagnosis and sent me to genetic specialists. The genetic counseling doctor looked me straight in the eye and said, "Well, maybe she can bag groceries someday at Target, if she's lucky."

I know, take your jaw off the floor.

"I love Target," I replied, "but I think managers get a better discount. So good day to you, Doctor. We won't be seeing you again." Mic drop! That's comic language but you get it.

When I got home I promptly took the binder full of all the worst-case scenarios the doctor had given me in her Beverly Hills office and threw it in the garbage. I made a choice that day to claim my belief in a better outcome for my daughter, and I decided to see where my faith in God could take us. Those early days were filled with doctors' appointments, therapy sessions, and oxygen tubes. I thank God for medical interventions and therapy.

It wasn't a quick or easy journey. Slowly but surely she hit her milestones. No, she didn't achieve them as lightning fast as her older sister had, but eventually she walked and talked and outgrew the need for oxygen. Her heart healed itself without surgery. Her lungs healed themselves. The doctor at UCLA cardiology told me when Ruby was six months old, "Well, your Jesus did it. I can't find any problems with her heart or lungs. Go home and only come see me for a social visit!"

Ruby never tired of hard work. I don't know a lot of babies and toddlers who had personal trainers, occupational therapists, and speech experts demanding their attention on a regular basis. And she never complained. When the therapists marveled at her progress, it was another opportunity for me to share the love and power of Jesus. Most of them cried, and one even came to church with us.

I took a lot of big leaps of faith, like enrolling her in regular pre-school, knowing she would either sink or swim. She did a little of both. Mostly she charmed everyone and ate other kids' lunches.

She no longer needed a lot of her therapies, but well-intentioned school officials told me I would be absolutely crazy to think about put-ting Ruby in a regular school like the one her sister was in. They said it wouldn't be possible because Lucy's school had no special needs classes or helpers, and the curriculum was quite advanced.

When Ruby was four years old, some of the kids in the fifth-grade class at Lucy's school, Redeemer Christian, partnered with their teacher, Miss Bradshaw, to get a desk with Ruby's name on it. I became friends with Miss Bradshaw when Lucy was in first grade at this school. Miss Bradshaw took it very seriously when I shared with her my heart's desire to have Ruby attend their school one day, knowing it would take a miracle. She rallied her class to pray for Ruby. They decided they would ask Ruby to visit their class, and they committed to pray over that desk and pray over her. The first time Ruby went to that class, I was moved to tears. Fifth-grade children were crying out to God to heal my little girl, asking Him to make it possible for her to attend this school…a school that believed in God and His promises. These kids did not stop. They spoke positive words over my girl. They spoke of hope and her success and bright future. They made her cards and drew pictures of her at Redeemer Christian. They prayed for an entire year, every single day in their classroom.

When it was time for Ruby to go to kindergarten, I took the leap of faith or insanity and enrolled her in Lucy's school. I arranged to have any speech therapy outside of school hours, and I believed God would take care of the rest. Thankfully, her class only had about 12 kids in it, and the teacher had been praying with expectation for Ruby's arrival. That year in kindergarten was truly awesome. Ruby thrived, and she started to read and write and sing songs. The whole experience was nothing short of a miracle. She was even in the spelling bee and got all her words right!

Fifth-grade children were crying out to God to heal my little girl, asking Him to make it possible for her to attend this school…a school that believed in God and His promises.

I was flying in each of those moments and giving God all the glory. She attended kindergarten graduation in a cap and gown, and she was even awarded Most Improved Student of the Year. There was no stopping her. And of course her Einstein sister didn't disappoint anyone with her highest honors and winning everything possible.

So first grade has been sort of a punch in the gut. Instead of realizing how far my little warrior has come, I'd let the anxiety of some ridiculous report cards and behaviors define her success or failure. It was my fault, not hers. She liked school, and she'd come a long way since September. She was writing and doing math, and her report cards had actually improved. It hadn't been a perfect or an easy year for us, especially since I am a single mom.

As I stood at the talent show, watching my little girl proclaim the promises of God over that audience, I was a mess. She said boldly,

"I walk by faith and *not* by sight."

"I set aside all that so easily besets me and I run this race with patience."

"Nothing is impossible for those who believe."

"I have the same spirit living in me that raised Christ from the dead!"

On and on she went, like a little preacher. She took her bow, and the audience went wild. In that moment I didn't think about posting this video on Facebook. I just thought about the massive, all-knowing, ever-loving God who formed my daughter in my womb. I thought about this very moment and all the moments to come—the good, the bad, and the ugly. I thought about the God who wrote all those verses in the Bible for me, for her, and for everyone in her life she would share them with. I remembered Jeremiah 29:11: "'I know the plans I have for you,' declares the Lord, 'plans to prosper you.'"

"Oh, God, I'm so sorry for freaking out over the details. I stopped listening to You and started listening to the world. I got on their scale and their timeline. I know we have miles to go with Ruby, and I won't stop believing for everything You have for her."

Fast-forward to May and the end-of-school honors chapel. I decided to honor her teacher with a nice gift and a card for her service for Ruby. I decided to focus on the positive, and I chose not to find fault with any of her negative words against my kid. I know taking the high road isn't always as satisfactory as trying to find justice when we feel wronged. But in this case it was the right thing to do. I was not in Ruby's class every day. For all I knew, she had been a total menace to society. But she made it. We made it, and that in itself was something to celebrate.

I sat there in chapel knowing Lucy would be receiving not only several academic awards but also awards for her physical strength in the PE Olympics Day. I got presents and cards for both my girls. I told them I was so extremely proud of them, for the people they are and for all they had accomplished. But it just broke my heart in a million pieces when Ruby said, "I'm next, Mommy!" after she saw some of the other first-graders going up for achievement awards

Now, these awards ceremonies are longer than the Oscars, so it's a bit hard to keep focus. And when Ruby's teacher came up on stage, I admit I wasn't really paying attention. She said, "This award for Most Improved Student of the Year goes to someone who has made me laugh more than I ever have in the classroom. I come into school, and she gives me a phrase or a look, and I crack up. This student is a joy to have in my class. She's improved in several areas, such as reading and spelling, and she loves to jump rope and eat at Chick-fil-A. The award goes to Ruby McGehee!"

You would have thought I was Halle Berry's mom when she won the Academy Award for Best Actress. I was a bawling mess. Ruby, however, calmly went up on the podium to the rousing cheers of her peers and accepted her award. It's like she knew she would get it. She received the same award last year, but in my wildest imagination I didn't think there was a chance she'd get it again in first grade. But she did. She crushed first grade! I failed, but she didn't.

I had to leave before the awards ceremony ended. I drove home elated and humbled, thanking God for what He'd done in my kid's life. You can imagine my shock later that day when Ruby came home with the award for "Queen of Reading" in her class, and she won *two*— not one, but *two*—medals in the PE Olympics! This kid placed in ball bounce and free throw. My faith was small, but God surprised me. Remember how the doctors said she would probably walk with leg braces or need a walker? #micdrop #teamJesus

---

I need to keep my eyes on Him, even when I'm down on the ground doing the ugly cry.

The Bible says that if I have faith the size of a mustard seed, I can tell a mountain to move into the sea. I suppose I did have that mustard seed faith, and so did others around me. God knew the plans He had for my child. I was reminded I can trust Him even when I can't see. I can trust Him even when it's hard. I can trust Him that He has bigger dreams in store for me and my family than I can even imagine. I just need to keep talking to Him. I need to keep my eyes on Him, even when I'm down on the ground doing the ugly cry. But hey, that's where you find the good candy—under your bed where you've been stashing it!

If you want to see more of my kids, feel free to check them out on all my social media pages. I regularly exploit them for comedy purposes, and I post Ruby's milestones because she's become such an encouragement to so many. I tell her story all over the world, and I often have her come on stage with me. She says, "My name is Ruby, and I'm a miracle." I've had people from countries far and wide contact me for prayer because they saw Ruby's story on YouTube.

Ruby Joy McGehee came into this world with a bang, and I look forward to seeing the next chapter. For now, it's summer and I plan on enjoying my kids and eating lots of chocolate and s'mores, because my bathing suit now has a skirt. Just like my mom's.

On a tangible note, I got Ruby an iPad for next year. We realized her brain works faster than her handwriting, so now she can use a typing app to complete her worksheets in class and do her homework. I hate to admit this, but typing is the future. I just want my kids to know how to sign a check so they can send me on cruises when they are supporting me in my old age.

And for your reference, here are a couple of the verses that got me through a lot of the trying times when we were battling for Ruby.

Praise the LORD, my soul,
and forget not all his benefits—
who forgives all your sins
and heals all your diseases (Psalm 103:2-3).

"For I know the plans I have for you," declares the Lord, "plans to prosper you not to harm you, plans to give you a hope and a future. Then you will call on me and come and pray to me, and I will listen to you" (Jeremiah 29:11-12).

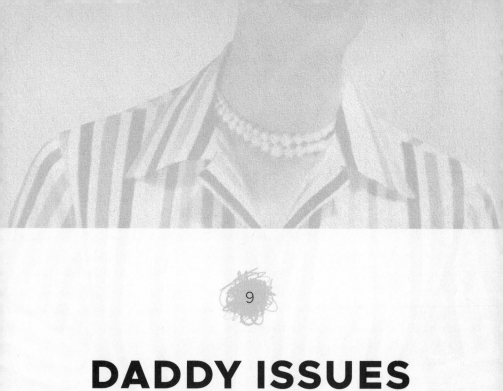

9

DADDY ISSUES

When I was in first grade at Dearborn Christian School, we had a Christmas bazaar fund-raiser. Ah…the joys of fund-raisers. Back then, parents couldn't just buy some wrapping paper and send a check. They were encouraged to have the whole family participate in this delightful event. Now, my mom, Barb, was Pinterest before Pinterest was a thing. She had spent many years perfecting knitting, sewing, macramé, rug hooking, decoupage, cake decorating, and anything else you could do with a needle. She learned fake flower arranging, microwave cooking with flare, and a host of other skills she picked up at the community center.

I, on the other hand, did not receive the crafty gene. Just ask my art teachers. Everything I did was a hot mess. I told them I was trying to emulate Picasso. They didn't buy it. This year, to my despair, each kid was ordered to come up with some kind of crafty object to sell at the kids' craft fair, and my six-year-old self wasn't having it. Looking back, my mom could have saved me, but I think she was at Jazzercise class. So I decided I would make pencil holders out of old frozen orange juice cans. I would take material from my mom's sewing scraps and glue them on the cans, certain I would create a trend of handmade original pencil cases. I'm sure these sell on Etsy today for quite a pretty penny.

I worked tirelessly in my basement on these creations. I convinced myself the glue seeping through the material was an added personal touch. I was very proud of my contribution. I think my mom made an entire house out of graham crackers and candy, and she donated it that year. I'm sure it was stunning. But I felt sorry for her, because who could compare to my one-of-a-kind, never-seen-before orange-juice-can-concentrate pencil holders? Sure, some kids made pot racks and some kids made necklaces out of macaroni. Hey, it was the '80s, and we didn't have craft kits to make jewelry or slime.

So the day of the fund-raiser arrived, and we loaded up Mom's masterpiece and mine. We jumped in our Ford Pinto and set off for a day of sales at the craft bazaar. We set up our table in the church basement, and I sat there beaming proudly at my contribution. None of my teachers or fellow students made any comments, but they were most likely jealous they hadn't come up with the idea.

At first people came by marveling at my mom's candy house, and they gave me a polite smile as they gazed at my amazing cases. But nobody was buying anything. I realized I needed to take it up a level. I put pencils *in* the pencil holders. Genius! And about 30 minutes later, it was like TJ Maxx on Black Friday. People of all ages were coming up to me, handing me quarter after quarter, buying up every single one of my pencil holders until I was completely *sold out*!

I made about $5. Was I surprised? No! Did my dad tell me these were the greatest pencil holders of all time and he wanted one for his office at the Ford Motor Company? Yes. Lucky for him I'd saved him one. But I made him pay. Hey, it was a fund-raiser!

I remember visiting my dad's office later that year, and there sitting proudly on his desk was the orange and green glue-covered pencil holder he'd bought from his daughter. Dad was proud of my success, and Mom was too. I had parents who thought I could be successful at anything I put my hand to. If I brought home macaroni glued on a stick, Mom displayed it in our kitchen. Whatever I did, they told me I was pretty much magnificent at it.

Now, some of you might call this type of parenting overly involved or giving false hope. Some of you may think they were outright lying. But I wouldn't change a thing. Their unadulterated confidence in me gave me the ability to be courageous and try new things. From the time I was five years old, I told them I was going to move to Hollywood and be a movie star. They said, "Sure you can. Just go to college first." And that's exactly what I did. Give or take 15 years.

I had parents who thought I could be successful at anything I put my hand to. If I brought home macaroni glued on a stick, Mom displayed it in our kitchen.

Many moons later, during some random conversation with my parents, I found out that the Great Pencil Holder Buy-Out of 1985 was masterminded by my own father. He was giving kids quarters and saying, "Hey, kid, I'll give you 50 cents if you go buy a pencil holder from that little girl over there. You can keep the change."

Yes, my father was rigging the sales. I laughed for days. Would I do that for my kids? No question!

And my dad's antics and surprises were only just beginning. When I was 15, I lived in a neighborhood that happened to house the hottest high school senior of all time. Let's call him Brian De Alexandres, because that's his real name. Back in my day, if you wanted to stalk a boy, you had to put in physical effort. We didn't have the Internet to do the search for us. You had to ride by his house on your bike a million times, hoping to catch him mowing the lawn in his gym shorts, and on a good day, maybe even shirtless.

Tracy Jambor and I were stealth spies on ten-speeds, and we were relentless in trying to get good intel that we could share with our friends on Monday morning. Brian and his neighbor friends went to Catholic Central High, and all of his friends were *hot*! We were measly sophomores, so they didn't fraternize with the likes of us. I wonder if they knew Tracy grew up to be a female bodybuilding modeling champion and has men swooning over her to this day. Puberty is a strange and wonderful thing!

Now, I don't remember really ever talking to the ever elusive Mr. De Alexandres at great length. I think I saw him at a neighborhood party or two, and I was probably choking on my cheese dip trying to get words out as he walked by. The cavernous divide between high school seniors and sophomores was just too wide to cross.

I don't think I can truly capture the magic of my sixteenth birthday or the astounding creativity of my dad, but I'll try. My dad told me to invite three of my girlfriends for an outing, and the activity was going to be a surprise. My dad was full of surprises and was known for epic birthday celebrations. Back then, bobbing for apples and a costume party was considered epic, but nonetheless, he always crushed it. (Today my kids are invited to parties where Celine Dion is the musical guest, puppies are flown in from Europe, and every kid leaves with an iPad! Am I kidding? Umm…kind of, but not really—it's LA!)

My dad led us up to his office building in downtown Detroit and told us we were being set up on blind dates by his very own personal dating service. Now, this was exciting, because at that point I had never been allowed to look at—much less date—a boy.

He gave a very elaborate comedy presentation and then four young gentlemen came out in wild-colored thrift store jackets with bags over their heads. Yes, bags over their heads. It was all very fun, and we were supposed to interview the candidates to find out who would be our best match. I whispered to my friends that I was pretty sure one of the guys was my family friend/like-a-cousin David. I figured David didn't mind getting all dressed up for my birthday, as he was used to my dad's hijinks.

After a few games, my dad lined us all up next to our dates for the evening. We were all giggling and being obnoxious and cracking jokes.

Then the time for the reveal came, and all the boys took off their thrift store jackets to reveal very nice suits. When the bags came off their heads, I was standing next to the *one and only Brian De Alexandres* and *three of his hot Catholic Central friends*. I knew one of them, Craig, from the neighborhood, but never in my wildest imagination did I think these boys would be there.

When the bags came off their heads, I was standing next to the one and only Brian De Alexandres and three of his hot Catholic Central friends.

Four teenage girls stood there silently with our jaws on the floor. I had no words, and for me, that's saying *a lot*! My dad looked at me and said with a smile and a wink, "Gotcha!"

We were then ushered away with the boys in a Ford Motor Company Lincoln Town Car limo to a dinner my dad paid for at the Hyatt Regency Hotel. What do I remember most about this night? The charming company? No, the unlimited candy at the dessert buffet! We all went home that night with pockets full of jelly beans.

Looking back, these guys were probably flattered when my dad asked them to be a part of my birthday. I'm sure they felt like rock stars. To this day I have no idea how my dad made it happen. It was crazy and unexpected, and now I can officially say my dad bought my first date. #Italianparenting

It was a birthday I'll never forget, and my dad continues to surprise and bless me to this day. He makes cards to encourage me to keep going in one of the toughest businesses out there. When I went off to college and later moved to LA, my dad made me a homemade card almost every single day. And all these years later, despite major health challenges, he still goes down to his basement and makes me cards and sometimes sticks a one-dollar bill in them. When I have a friend who is going through a tough time, I'll phone my dad, and he'll make one of his cards. (On a side note I must mention my mother has also gotten into the homemade card business, and we've been blessed on all sides with real mail in our mailbox, not just bills.)

I know you could be reading this and thinking, *Well, it's easy for her to talk about how great dads are. Her dad was doting and adoring, and mine wasn't even there. Or when he was there, he was less than kind—or worse.* That stinks. I mean it. I don't think anyone should have to go through any kind of abuse. If you've had struggles with your dad, it might be hard for you to picture a God up there who loves you like a father. Maybe you cringe every single time you even hear the words "Father's love" because it seems like a sick joke to you. You got the short end of the stick with your earthly dad, and now you're expected to buy into the fact that your Father God up in heaven was supposedly looking out for you the whole time? If you question that in church circles, do you fear you'll seem ungrateful or lacking in faith?

I'm here to tell you one thing from personal experience. God can take it. He can take your anger, your rage, your disappointment—all of it. What if the absence of a father figure is the root of your bad choices in your relationships and now you've ended up in a bad situation? And the world has told you it's your fault? Who can be there to help you sort all that out? For starters, it's not a bad idea to talk to a counselor, a pastor, or a good friend you can trust.

If this chapter brings up some old feelings you haven't really ever dealt with, I believe it's a good thing you're reading it. Maybe God is speaking to you right now. Yes, you. You know who you are. Maybe you're reading this book in the bathtub, and you're kind of crying right now, but you're trying to hold it in. It's okay, my friend. Let's think together about how we can help you work through at least some of these feelings. I'm not a professional, so just remember this advice is free and you get what you pay for.

Your dad—or someone in a fatherlike position—may have hurt you by leaving or by staying and by not being the loving dad you needed. What are you supposed to do with that? Stop listening to Oprah and the world, who tell you there is some therapy book that will fix it all in 30 days. Don't believe the lie that you're a strong, independent woman and you can just get over it. Don't listen when they say you don't need God to comfort you through all this pain.

Maybe you are listening to Satan and the many lies he's probably tried to tell you your whole life. He lied to you about your value. He lied about your worth. He told you that you'd never be deserving of a healthy man to love you, so why even try? He tempted you with things to numb the pain: food, alcohol, drugs, or men. Maybe you gave in to those temptations and you figured out they weren't all they promised to be. The high didn't last that long, the guy left you, and unhealthy choices just added up to more hurt. No one here is judging you. God loves you no matter what your past looks like. This is between you and God. It's okay! You're okay, even if you don't feel okay right now. I say you are *going to be okay*. You have the power to change your circumstances, starting right now.

If you're taking the time to think about some of this stuff, you can take the time to think about the fact that God has better plans for your future than your past. But you have to take the first step. Does the thought of talking to God scare you? Try reading the Bible. You'll see that people talked to God all the time, even when they couldn't see Him.

God has better plans for your future than your past.

I take a lot of comfort in reading the psalms, because they are filled with verses of David flat-out complaining and lamenting to God, ranting and raving in total anger or despair. Did God turn His back on David? Did God say, "You are an adulterer and a murderer. Who are you to complain to Me like this"? No, God listened to His child cry out. And God called David a man after His own heart. Because that's what a father says about the child he loves. He comforted David in his sorrow and fear and was with him every step of the way.

Sometimes well-meaning Christians try to tell me all about the power of the tongue—you reap what you sow, and every word you utter has power. I've literally been told before if I pray the wrong way I'm going to make my situation worse because I said "something negative."

And yes, as a prayer warrior, I believe our words have power. But I refuse to believe God doesn't allow us to have real, frank, tearful, put-your-head-in-your-pillow-and-scream conversations. Or else He wouldn't have kept the book of Psalms in the Bible. David was real with his Father God. And that's what God wants from you…your pain, your feelings, your fears, and anything else you have to share. You are a daughter after His own heart.

I suspect if you had the chance to have a one-on-one talk with God you might hear Him say:

My daughter, My daughter, I love you more than you could ever imagine.

All those times when you were hurting and feeling alone, I saw every tear. I cried with you. You couldn't see Me, but I was there. You couldn't hear Me, but I was speaking. I was telling you that you are strong. I was whispering that you will not be in this situation forever and that I made you to be a fighter. You didn't know it, but I was preparing you for the exact place you are right now. It was hard, but you made it through. Every battle you faced I knew would make you more of a warrior, even though it broke My heart to see you hurting. I have plans to overcome everything the enemy throws at you.

You, My daughter, are beautiful. I've watched you every single second of your life, even in the times you felt most alone. I adore you. I relish in watching you navigate this world. Someday you will be with Me in paradise, but until then, I want you to give Me the chance right now to heal your heart. Will you let Me?

I love you so much that I gave My only child to pay the ultimate painful price so you wouldn't have to carry that broken heart forever. A better day is coming and an ultimate destination exists where you and I will spend eternity together. But in the meantime I wrote these words for you. Put your name in them: "Come to me, all you who are weary and burdened, and I will give you rest. Take my yoke upon you and learn from me, for I am gentle and humble in heart, and you will find rest for your souls" (Matthew 11:28-29).

Write those words on your bathroom mirror and repeat them every day, because they are a personal promise from Me to you. You can find rest. Now, My child, it's up to you to believe it. All I ask is that you give Me all the pain that's been a shackle to you for so long. Give it to Me, and know how it feels to walk free. I can carry it for you.

I can help you do the unthinkable: forgive. If you choose to let Me help you forgive in My strength, not yours, you can find the joy you've been searching for. What do you have to lose, My child?

I love you so much, My darling. I am your true Father. I am the One who formed you in your mother's womb. I picked out every chromosome, gene, and hair on your little head. I love you with wild abandon. Nothing you can do or have done can ever make Me love you any less. Humans can't promise you that, because their love can be conditional. But I am not a human. I am the God who created the heavens and the earth, and I care about every day that you have been on this planet. That will never stop.

Will you let Me love you?

Your Father,
God

Here are some other verses to hold on to. I'm a big fan of posting promises of Scripture all around my house. My bathroom has many of them, because that is the place I can sometimes be the stillest.

> He gives strength to the weary
> and increases the power of the weak.
> Even youths grow tired and weary…
> but those who hope in the LORD
> will renew their strength.
> They will soar on wings like eagles;
> they will run and not grow weary,
> they will walk and not be faint (Isaiah 40:29-31).

> He heals the brokenhearted
> and binds up their wounds (Psalm 147:3).

10

DEAR DIARY, OH DIARY

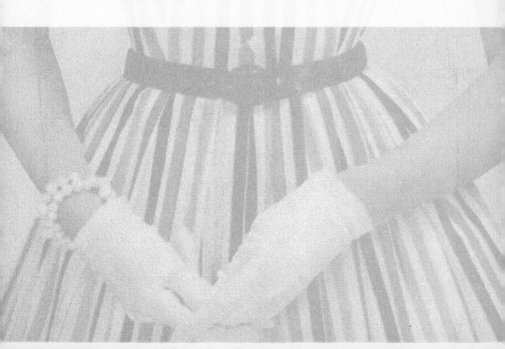

D ear reader, I struggled over whether to include the following chapter or not. It's quite revealing and embarrassing. If my mom reads it, I could be in trouble. (No, I'm not kidding.) But I talk about being the kind of person who's not afraid to take that "Insta-perfect Christian mask" off, so here it goes. The names have been changed to protect me from getting sued. Except Anthony Policello. I'm seriously looking for him! He's in Michigan. If you happen to find him, let me know. I think we have some unfinished business to attend to.

I often hear Christian speakers share powerful testimonies of how God delivered them from a life of drug use or addiction. I never judge them. I'm always inspired by their journey. I don't have that dramatic a testimony, but God did have to deliver me from being an idiot. I mean, a complete hormonal idiot, from the age of 16 till about 29. Should I share this info with you? Will we find some spiritual meaning in the fact that I was boy-crazy as a teenager and obsessed with men and didn't learn my lesson until I was almost 30? They say it's not healthy to dwell in the past, especially past sinful behavior. But I think sometimes it's a good idea to take a look back and see how far we've come. As long as my mother and my children never know about it.

Sometimes it's a good idea to take
a look back and see how far we've
come. As long as my mother and
my children never know about it.

So, Barb, Lucy, Ruby: if you are reading this book, please kindly skip to the next chapter. I'm sure it's more suitable.

Okay, kids. Let's dive in, shall we?

I was cleaning out my garage today. I was throwing away old bread boxes, deflated soccer balls, halogen lights, and toys my kids would never know were missing when I stumbled upon a box of my old diaries. Now, I've kept a diary literally since I could write, which might have been first grade. If you don't believe me, check out my first book, *Guys Like Girls Named Jennie*, and you'll see. I published most of them. And my ex-boyfriends? I used their real names. Just like the Bible does!

I had a torrid affair in third grade with Anthony Policello that was well documented, one he did not know about because it existed solely in my mind. I have to admit, these diaries from third grade are pretty hysterical. I even took to reading them out loud in my web series on YouTube: "Diary of a Mad 3rd Grader." People seemed to get a kick out of my love life. Little did I know when I was eight I'd be writing about my relationships, or lack thereof, for many years to come. Mostly people laugh at me, but this is how I support my two lovely children. My pain = their gain!

Before I got engaged some years ago, I took some of the more scandalous journals from my early to midtwenties and threw them away. Before you freak out about my past behaviors, let's just clarify that my definition of *scandalous* is pretty mild compared to some. But hey, we all have our own journey. And like my pastor used to say, "You were just working on your testimony!"

Mom, stop reading now. Seriously, Barb, it's for the best!

On this day in the garage, I found a little blue diary with a silver lock, with big letters on the front spelling out the word *Confidential*. When I opened it, I found a list of numbers, and next to each number was the name of a guy. This diary was from my freshman year in college, and this list was quite a bit longer than I remembered, though I will not tell you how long this list was. (Okay, if you email me, I might.) I started reading at the beginning, and I recognized names of boys and men I had either dated, had torrid long-distance affairs with (back when long-distance calling cost 40 cents a minute), or even had long-term relationships with up until college. I think the list started with the first guy I ever loved: John Schneider from *Dukes of Hazzard*. I really peaked at Bo Duke, and then it kind of went downhill from there. Scott Baio and Corey Feldman from *Goonies* were also on the list, both of whom I've had the pleasure of meeting later in life. I hadn't always included last names. Some were listed such as "Josh— Beta frat dude," "Marcos—hot Latin guy in my NYU dorm," and "Pat—Hawaii surfer guy."

I don't know why I needed to write such a list. Was I Carrie Bradshaw?

I put down the journal and saved reading my descriptions for after my kids were asleep. I knew it would be entertaining and laughable. I always was a very expressive writer. That night, after I put the kids to bed, I sat in my favorite comfy chair in my bedroom with a cup of hot tea and began to read. As I read the first page, I started choking on my chamomile tea and it trickled out of my mouth and down my nightgown. Yes, it was hot.

I don't know how to explain exactly what I was feeling. It was like an out-of-body experience. I recognized the handwriting, but surely I was not the one who had written these things. On these pages was every single detail of my love life in college—and not much else. I think I went to classes, but there was no record of it. I think I got an education and learned some things, but you would never know it. What you would know were the day-to-day, night-by-night exploits of a girl on mission—and not from God!

I make fun of kids today when I say, "Well, at least all the stupid things I did happened before Facebook, so there is no photographic evidence. All their dumb stuff is in cyberspace forever!" Why on earth would I record all these sordid emotional details—good, bad, and mostly ugly—for all to possibly see? Did my mother read these? Chills went down my spine. If she did read these and the 27 other diaries, how did she keep from sending me to a convent? Or off to the military? (The military wouldn't have helped. I love soldiers!) Or for deliverance prayer? How did she sleep at night?

I mean, who was this girl? Boy crazy doesn't even begin to cover it. Boy obsessed? No boundaries whatsoever? Needy? That's good for a start! And the worst part is that I wasn't even interested in one guy at a time. I would be writing how much in love/lust I was with my so-called boyfriend, and then I'd turn the page and read all about me dancing to "Tainted Love" on the bar at the Beta fraternity party with John Heller. And to top it off, I didn't even drink. I did all of this stuff sober!

I mean, who was this girl?

My girlfriends and sorority sisters would lament, "I was so drunk last night. I can't believe I was dancing like that. But, Kerri, your karaoke solo to Michael Jackson's 'Pretty Young Thing' was insane! What were you drinking?"

My reply: "Um…Sprite."

As I read my journal, I didn't know whether to laugh, cry, or get matches to burn the evidence of my bad choices. This wasn't quite as charming as my diaries from third grade, chronicling my unrequited love of Anthony Policello.

Then, as I was reading, I was startled when a little voice popped up next to me. "What are you reading, Mommy? Wanna cuddle?"

I almost jumped off my chair. My daughter looked like the ghost from Christmas Past in the dimly lit bedroom. "Oh, nothing, honey. Nothing… Nothing you will ever see," I muttered under my breath as Lucy tried to take a glance.

"What does *confidential* mean, Mom?" she asked.

"Mmm, it means not for kids! Go to bed!"

I felt as though I was reading some R-rated novel that I needed to hide under my bed before I got caught. Okay, maybe in reality it wasn't that bad, but did I have to be such an overly expressive writer? Did I not know the power of editing? This was horrifying.

Then my ten-year-old pranced back in the room and said, "One more thing, Mom. Can we talk about guys? I think I'm old enough to know. My friends are talking about dating and stuff, and you said I could ask you anything, so can we talk?"

It was now 8:40 p.m., and I gulped down my tea and did my best to shove her back into her room with a promise of that discussion happening in the next few days or weeks. I was hoping that by morning she would forget she'd asked. I mean, this kid still believes in the Tooth Fairy, so do I have to explain men to her? Oh, wait. Maybe I won't have to. I can just hand her this journal and say, "Well, just *don't do this!* Don't be this girl!"

I kept reading page after page after page about this guy or that guy and how this one was "different" from all the rest. I was totally helplessly in love with _____ (fill in the blank). I did enjoy reading about my on-again/off-again romance with Brad McKinley. (Name changed to protect the guilty.) He was so smart. He got a perfect SAT score and a full ride to the University of Michigan. He aspired to be president. He said dating me was bringing down his grade point average, but he didn't care. (I've always been such an uplifting influence on my male partners. I should be proud.) Well, now he works in the

White House, and he is very high up in government. I'd love to get his address and say, "Hello, sir. I have some information about you I think you'd find quite interesting. Send me $50,000 or I sell it to TMZ!"

We threw around the words *I love you* and *soul mate* quite easily, and I was all in until the next Mr. Right popped up on the dance floor with Prince's "Purple Rain" in the background.

As I kept reading story after story, I saw a pattern:

Girl meets Boy.

Girl dances with Boy to cheesy '80s love song.

Boy professes undying love and adoration for Girl.

Girl and Boy make out to cheesy '80s love song on dance floor.

Girl drops everything and obsesses about Boy.

Boy and Girl continue the drama cycle, exchanging mix tapes, flowers, and phone calls until Boy tires of Girl or Girl meets New Boy at frat party.

Repeat!

Gross, I tell you! Gross. If I was counseling this girl right now, I would hit her upside the head and say, "Snap out of it! You're being an idiot! You don't know what love is. You just need Jesus! Didn't you get enough love as a child?"

Now, I could say that all of this stemmed from the lack of a father's love, but in my case, that would be a bald-faced lie. My dad worshiped the ground I walked on. He said any man who didn't fall in love with his daughter was blind! So I guess we'll chalk this one up to the fact that my mother didn't breastfeed me as a baby. Yeah, that's why I need so much attention!

I loved meeting new people, especially handsome dark-haired, brown-eyed new people. I don't think these guys had any idea what they were in for. Sometimes, after many hours of dancing, these dudes would use whatever line they could think of to get me alone. "Do you want to go up to my room and see my goldfish? Do you want to go somewhere and talk?" Okay, so maybe I was a bit naïve, but I took their requests literally. I would go to some strange destination where I could have easily been murdered and chopped into little pieces. And we would talk. I'm not kidding. I could talk to a goldfish for three hours if I had to. I have the gift of gab. But all this time I thought the guy was falling in love with me when now I think he was falling asleep. I would stay at the frat house or dorm room or wherever until the wee hours of the morning, discussing pretty much every subject on the planet.

I think they were probably trying to think of a polite way to get me to go home, but they were so confused they just went along with it. Besides, people like to talk about themselves, and my psychologist dad told me to always ask questions. I would then go home and record all the details of my newfound love and how we really made a "special connection." There was Eric who serenaded me outside my window. Mike who wrote me poems. Andy who was sweet as pie, which is why I dumped him quite quickly.

According to these written records, all of these nights did not end with such nunlike behavior. Gross! Gross! Gross! There is no other word for it. The whole thing was stupid and dramatic and heartbreaking—and thrilling if you're into youthful angst.

Each page was more shocking than the one before. But what killed me was when I would write things like: "Partied like a rock star at the Beta house last night. I met Andy and he is super hot and has six-pack abs! I think God has great plans for my life! Maybe I should go to church or pray more. I am so blessed." Or: "Thought about going to church, but it was too cold. Had lunch with Bill instead."

Wow. All that Christian upbringing and ten years of Bible school sure shined through like a beacon of light. More like a spotlight on the dance floor.

I *was* kind of awesome with my dance abilities, I must say. I had these skintight red plaid pants I wore a lot, and if the fashion police had been around back then, I would have been arrested for indecent use of plaids! What was I trying to be, a bagpiper? My hair was as big as a Ms. Texas contestant, and my blue mascara shimmered in the night air along with my glitter eye shadow. I must confess: in my possession right now is my Sephora blue mascara and glitter eye shadow, because, well…everything comes back, baby!

But back to my story. I couldn't even finish the diary that night because it was emotionally exhausting for me to relive that year in my life, now referred to as the "Debauchery Chronicles." Maybe you're reading this and it's triggering memories of your more stupid decisions. As a gift to you, let me completely validate you: *no one* was dumber than I was. No one was more of a love/lust-sick puppy on more occasions than I was. It's just not possible. Where did I get all that energy? Maybe all the cortisol and endorphins were keeping me going. Or was it the Red Bull and Coke? (The drink, not the drug.)

As a gift to you, let me completely validate you: no one was dumber than I was.

As I lay in bed that night, thinking about what I had just discovered and read, I felt so many conflicting emotions running through me. On the one hand it all did sound kind of exotic and exciting in some way. I was the leading lady in my own romantic comedy series. It had to be a TV show—there were just too many men for one movie. It's as though I was Meg Ryan or Reese Witherspoon or Julia Roberts (not *Pretty Woman*) in my own mind. And it occurred to me that all those movies I grew up with had the exact same behavior modeled for me.

When I was a little girl and then a teenager, I'd watch those romcoms over and over, and every single time the story had a happy ending. The bad boy changed his wild ways to win the girl's heart. The dramatic fights turned into passionate makeup sessions, and no matter how many romantic adventures the leading couple had, both with and without each other, they *always* ended up together, committed and happy at the end.

Deep down inside every one of us is a little girl who wants a movie happy ending in real life.

I know we think we always want to find out what happened to our favorite movie characters, but do we really? If they resembled anything like the lives of the stars who played them, we'd be hearing about infidelities, lawsuits, child custody battles, and divorce. But Hollywood keeps making these types of movies, and we keep watching them. That's because deep down inside every one of us is a little girl who wants a movie happy ending in real life. I guess I just took matters into my own hands about a million times too many, and I tried to literally force some movie magic into my life. I picked guys who were all too willing to play the role of leading man/hero or "tragic rebel/needing to be rescued."

That night in my room I dealt with an exorbitant amount of guilt, shame, and disgust for my behaviors. My exploits could be seen as a bit comedic, but to me they were awful. And maybe those choices had set me up for making more bad choices. Maybe my life could have been so different if *I Kissed Dating Goodbye* (Christian book circulated late '90s). My book could have been called *I Gave Making Out a Chance!: An Unauthorized Biography.*

Boys were like a sport to me. I was a champion and a loser, all at the same time. I was so sad to see that it looked to me as though I never learned any lessons. I never vowed not to make these mistakes again, and I never, ever recorded feeling even a little bit guilty. Where was the

Holy Spirit in my life back then? I don't think I even knew the phrase "Listen to the Holy Spirit." I clearly knew the phrase "Don't get caught!"

The next day, I consulted a couple of trusted friends about my recent diary reading and asked them what they would do. Of course anyone who was a mom said, "Burn the evidence and lie to your kids like our moms did to us!" One friend said I should take this as proof of how much I've grown and how far I've come. I was still very conflicted.

Reading all that got me thinking about the Proverbs 31 Woman. The whole chapter is about what a hard worker, a loving mother, and a devoted wife she is. But don't you wish there was a little morsel included about her life before she got married? I'm not saying she was best friends with the "woman at the well," who was quite well known by the fellas. But was she that exceptional before she got married and had kids? Did she have a wild phase? Maybe she hung around Delilah in the early days. We'll never know. But the Bible is filled with people with a past, and God still told them their sins were forgiven, wiped away, and they were white as snow. Why do I have such a hard time accepting that part of the Bible is as true for me as it was for them?

I think one of the devil's biggest tactics—at least in my life—is persistent false guilt and shame. I know I've told God many times I was sorry for all the nonsense that went on back then. So why was I right back there, wallowing in my sin? It was as though the devil was whispering in my ear, "You call yourself a Christian leader and a role model for your girls? Wait till they find out about all of this. They are never going to listen to you. You should stop what you're doing because you're not qualified to be anybody's role model with a past like yours." Now listen, that little speech would be all too easy to believe. It makes sense, doesn't it? I was raised by two perfect parents who never sinned and by teachers who were flawless. (At least that's the story I was told.)

Okay, you are *not* going to believe this! I was staying at my mom and dad's house in Georgia while I was working on this book. I was writing this chapter one night, and the next morning my mom said to me in that sweet Southern drawl, "I read your chapter."

"Which one?" I asked.

"The one you left open on my computer."

I promise you, even though I'm a grown woman, my face turned purple and I was prepared to get grounded. She then proceeded to tell me I should not include this chapter in my book because it makes a bad impression. She said, "I thought you were writing a Christian book." (This is coming from a woman who has yet to confess to not being a virgin.)

I love my mom dearly, but she was raised to be a beautiful prim and proper lady by another beautiful prim and proper lady. They were taught to hide or burn the evidence of anything that even appeared to be improper. And it works for her. All her friends are lovely and sweet, and they don't find it appropriate to air their dirty laundry to each other, or so it seems.

My mom and I have had many a battle about the fact that she thinks I overshare with my friends. Oh, and I'm not allowed to use the word *dysfunctional* about my family in my act. (Even if I'm joking!) But I am not like my mom. I have to share with my friends. I'm a verbal processor, and besides, therapy is expensive. I'd owe my friend Cathy about $5 million by now if she charged me by the hour for counseling.

I'm grateful I can be open and honest about my struggles. How can I grow and learn if every time I mess up I keep it a secret? Wouldn't all that eventually bubble up inside me and then manifest itself in some bad way? Not all secrets are meant to be shared, and I respect that. But maybe God has called us to work on ourselves and help others so we can relate to their mishaps and struggles. Some of the best advice I've ever received has come from people who looked me straight in the eye and could honestly say, "I get it. I've been there!"

I didn't seek that kind of advice growing up. I was too busy trying to sit at the right lunch table and have the most amazing bangs. There was no room for slipping up. It was eat or be eaten. Thank you, Northville High School, for proving to me I can survive any battle.

College was no different. I had friends, but we were too young and ambitious to stop and admit there were any problems in our relationships. I was a musical theater major, after all. Anything could be solved with a tap dance and a show tune!

Maybe God has called us to work on ourselves and help others so we can relate to their mishaps and struggles.

When I moved to California, I started going to this little weird church where people wore jeans and Hawaiian shirts and raised their hands during the singing time. They didn't have pews, and the Catholic in me didn't know where to kneel. And because of my mother's influence, I was in a skirt and pearls. I didn't seem to fit in, but they had potluck dinners, so I kept coming back. I felt like a fraud every Sunday, as though I was faking it. But they didn't seem to mind. I wanted to make friends and become one of them…you know, the good people—the "real" Christians. These people were really in love with God, and they weren't afraid to be open about it. I envied them.

I felt caught between two worlds and tugged in two directions. I even dragged my boyfriend at the time to church with me. He said he'd go if I drove. We eventually broke up, but I kept going on Sundays and I never stopped.

It's been a wild ride ever since with God and different church homes and different paths taken. I've learned a lot, and I'm not the person who wrote that journal anymore. But I think it would be wrong to forget her, because reading between the lines of those pages, I saw a lost little girl looking for love in all the wrong places. What she really needed was a bona fide love connection with a Savior who would be the lover of her soul and never leave her. I finally found that later in my life, but it was a crooked path to get there. I'm not going to be ashamed and condemn myself, because I know I am forgiven. And maybe my story can help someone else.

If you found a journal from some of your worst times, how would you react? Does thinking about your past bring up any unresolved feelings of guilt or shame? What if five years from now you found a detailed account about your life and actions right now? Is there anything burning on your heart that you need to give to God, once and for all? You can, you know, with one prayer. Just pray:

Dear God,

Your Word says You remember my sins no more. I repent of _____. I ask You to forgive me and release me from any guilt the devil has tried to burden me with. I am a new creation in Christ Jesus because of the cross. Please help me live in that freedom on a daily basis, communing with You. I choose to believe Your truth about me. I am valuable and worthy to serve in Your army of believers.

ADVICE FOR RAISING CHILDREN

From Kerri's Mom, Barbara

1. Don't miss any opportunity to tell your children how good they have things. After all, you had to walk five miles uphill barefoot in the snow to get to school every day. They get chauffeured to school, only walk a block, or better yet, get to stay home and be homeschooled.

2. Do not let a four-year-old tell you what she will or will not wear. If she doesn't want to wear dresses or matching colors at that age, think what she will be wearing when she's 15. She has to learn now that it's not appropriate to wear white after Labor Day.

3. Do not let your child tell their grandmother—or any older person, for that matter—that she has squishy skin. Getting old is challenging enough.

4. Caution your child not to point out to someone (especially in a loud voice in the ladies dressing room at the swimming pool) that he or she is fat. It's okay for an adult not to be able to touch their toes.

5. Teach your children respect for adults, and that means saying "yes, ma'am" and "yes, sir" if you are in the South and "yes" and "no" in other parts of the country. "Yeah" and "naw" are not acceptable ways to address adults.

6. Be very careful about which movies and television shows your children watch, as they may imitate what they see. If you find them with a cup sitting on the street in front of your house begging, you know they should not have watched *Oliver Twist*.

7. Teach them there is a time and place for make-believe and it is not when you are traveling through TSA at the airport.

Telling the guard your name is Beyoncé, which does not match your ticket, is not okay.

8. Teach them to see the funny side of life early on. It will serve them well.

9. Teach them that it is not appropriate to say, "Lord, get the wrinkles off this woman's face right now. In Jesus's name" when they are praying with an older woman.

10. When all seems lost, send them to Grandma's house so they can be spoiled and sugared up and then sent home.

11

THE GRASS
IS ALWAYS
GREENER, EVEN
WHEN IT'S FAKE

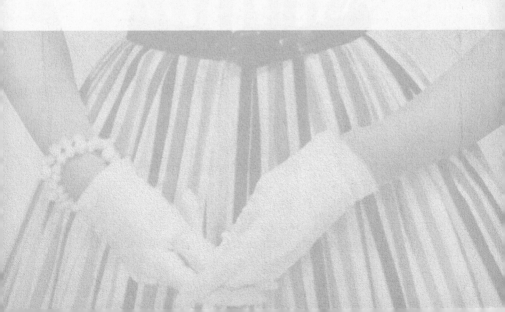

Hello, my fair reader friend. How are you enjoying our little journey so far? Have I convinced you that I am a bigger mess than you are? Do you feel better about your life, your faith, and your domestic abilities? I hope so, or else why am I writing down all this horribly embarrassing stuff?

I've had an interesting life working in Hollywood (the land of fruits and nuts) and in Christian ministry all over the country. Sometimes I don't know what's real and what's fake. I don't think social media has done us any favors. I often forget what I really looked like before Instagram filters were invented. Sometimes I go to take a photo with my phone and I accidentally have the lens pointed at me and I get this gruesome reality check of my face close up. It's like watching a horror movie. You can't turn away fast enough. But sometimes the lighting is just perfect, that crema filter is on point, and I look like I just came out of the hair salon. I have that "messy hair don't care," "I just woke up this way" look, and all is well with the world. #nofilter #notreally #everyonefilters #iftheysaytheydonottheyarelying!

I realize the business I have chosen to make my life's work is probably the worst on the planet for my self-esteem. As a comedian, here's the cycle: I get a job, I go do the job, the job is over, I feel as if I've been fired, and then I have to start all over again. I bare my soul in front of a crowd of total strangers who might rather be gathering around a chocolate fountain. I can see in their eyes that the Christians wish I were Beth Moore and the non-Christians wish I were Amy Schumer.

I realize the business I have chosen to make my life's work is probably the worst on the planet for my self-esteem.

Not only do I want them to love me, but I also want them to have a physical, audible reaction to what I'm saying, such as laughter, claps, tears, or all three. If I don't get one of these responses, I feel I have not done my job. If I'm really good, someone will spit up their food.

Then I am vulnerable enough to meet and greet said strangers after my performance, and I get to hear their one-on-one opinions about the life story I just shared. People will tell me they don't agree with my theology, and though they know I meant well, I have upset them and they believe I am dead wrong on the points I was trying to make. Sometimes they give me suggestions on how to improve my material. But on special occasions I will get an email telling me how much my show and testimony meant to someone and blessed him or her.

I put myself out there, creating personal content for YouTube and social media, and then I get to read all the comments of what people like or don't like about the videos. Some people are quite eloquent with their words, posting things like "Not good" or "Stupid." And my personal favorite: "Women aren't funny!"

Now, here's the joke. (Get it? Joke? I'm a comedian?) Ninety-nine percent of the feedback I've gotten for the past 12 years has been loving and wonderful and positive. But for some reason I'm conditioned to focus on the few and far between negative commentaries that get ingrained in my head. One time I was doing a national conference and after the sessions all the speakers and performers received anonymous feedback from the audience. One person said, "She was funny but chubby." I happened to be six months pregnant at the time, and I was talking about it in my act!

As a comedian, the term *embarrassing moment* takes on a whole new meaning. Everything in my life becomes material, and sometimes it happens right in the moment on stage between me and the audience. One time I had some surgery and was on pain meds for a few days. I had to do a show so my husband (we were married at the time) drove me to the venue, which happened to be a church. I took my pain meds before I went on stage, and that's the last thing I remember. As the legend goes, I did 11 minutes on the spirituality of the singer Prince and how he didn't get enough credit in the Christian community. (I don't think I was invited back.)

I have a million of these "precious moments" on stage that I promised would be in a book someday. Well, here we are! I've had wardrobe malfunctions, like the time my skinny jeans busted open on stage because I was three months pregnant and had no business wearing them. Ah, vanity. After I had that baby, I think I wore maternity jeans for a year.

The journey I've been on in comedy for all these years has been remarkable, to say the least. It's been filled with highs and lows and higher highs and lower lows. Being married to a comedian and having two kids while touring the country is a book unto itself. Going through a divorce with that same comedian is a whole other book.

It's my job to provide joy and laughter to my audiences no matter what my life might look like on the inside. The first rule of comedy is "never let 'em see you sweat." Translation: My problems are not their problems, and the show must go on. In over a decade of touring, you can imagine I've had my share of tragedies come up in my life. But I've still managed to get my job done through the grace of God, Coca-Cola, and Sun Chips.

People ask me how I keep up this rigorous work schedule, raise two kids, and not go insane. I guess I never stopped to think about the pace of things. I was too busy surviving and climbing that never-ending ladder going who-knows-where. When I moved to Hollywood I had definite goals in mind. I wanted to marry Matt Damon and be on TV. Well, one out of two ain't bad.

Such a huge motivating factor for me in pursuing a show business career was desiring to experience that feeling of "arrival." Aren't most of us constantly feeling as though we are in a race but we have no idea where the finish line is? Is it when we have the perfect job, house, car, family, dress size? I wanted all of those things and more. And to some degree I had all of them. (Minus the perfect car. I drove my Volvo for 11 years until it finally started talking to me. It was saying, "Let me die! Please let me die!") But to all those around me, I looked like I had "it" going on. I was married to a fellow funny man who loved Jesus. He toured with me, and he understood the madness of my job. I had a house near the beach in LA, two great kids, and a job I loved. I was invited to parties, hosted red carpets and award shows, and found a way to fuse my passion for the gospel with my passion for making people laugh. I was able to write books and scripts, and I had the opportunity to use my creative gifts on a daily basis. What's not perfect about that? If you read about me on the back of a book cover or in a magazine interview, you will only hear about all the laughter in my life. Because really, who's going to write an article about a comedian experiencing sorrow? That doesn't sell!

**Aren't most of us constantly feeling
as though we are in a race but we
have no idea where the finish line is?**

But in this day and age, when we the public have had the chance to peer behind the curtain and see celebrities struggling with depression, it's hopefully been an eye-opener to realize the grass isn't always so green on the other side of the fence. I've had the privilege of meeting and working with major celebrities, so I've seen them off stage. It would break your heart to hear the stories of addiction and sadness and despair they've expressed behind closed doors. Did you know the comedy clubs have a special phone list for certain celebrities who come in there a lot? The list includes the people to call when they get too drunk, especially if they become belligerent or end up crying in the corner. If I told you who these people were, you'd be shocked. (Email me. I can be bribed.)

But even publicly you've seen famous people confess to difficulties in their life. I saw a documentary called *Dying Laughing* in which comedian Amy Schumer said, "I'm not altogether happy most of the time." This girl is on top of the world with her career, but there is a deep sense of melancholy about her. "What more could she want?" we ask. I am reminded of the sad clown you see in paintings. A lot of comedians are actually sad clowns who just want to be around laughter because they need it so much. I can assure you, most of us didn't choose this job because we had a normal childhood! Jim Carrey, one of my favorite sad clowns, said, "I wish everyone could get rich and famous and have everything they ever dreamed of so they would know that's not the answer."

Recently we've seen a rise in public suicides of the very rich and famous. As I am writing this, just this week we lost one of the world's best fashion designers and a major TV personality to suicide. Didn't they look like they were living "la dolce vita"? If asked, I might have traded places with them. But we don't know what their lives were really like. We only saw them through the rose-colored glasses Hollywood PR agents provided us with.

The same is true with people we see up on the pulpits in public ministry. They don't usually share what is going on behind the scenes before they step up to deliver their message. They could be battling an illness, caring for sick family members, or any number of things. But they still get up and preach the message of hope. Thinking about that gets me pondering the Proverbs 31 Woman. I wonder if she ever felt jealous of her friends. Did she want to be queen like Esther or have a better place to live?

I'm not writing this book so I can tell you sob stories about how hard my life is. But I am writing to share about a constant struggle of mine, which is plain old-fashioned jealousy. I mean, it's bad. Like breaking-the-ten-commandments-every-day bad. I've definitely coveted my neighbor's everything about a million times. I bet I'm not alone. Social media isn't helping either. Just once I wish we all had to be like Jim Carrey's character in the movie *Liar Liar*, where he couldn't lie. We'd have to post with 100 percent honesty on social media. Unfiltered. Instead of "messy hair, don't care." Or, "Love these precious mornings having quiet time with my kids before school and my workout." Or, "What a way to start my week, with joy and healthy choices!"

I wish I had the courage to post the "real" reality of my life.

I woke up late today tired. My neck hurt from clenching my jaw. My TV was on all night and there is a random child sprawled across my bed. Immediately my mind started spinning out on all the things I had to do today that didn't get done yesterday. I threw my hair in a bun, forgot to brush my teeth, and pulled on the sweatpants that nobody saw me in yesterday. I looked homeless. I fed my kids some high-fructose-corn-syrup excuse for a breakfast, yelled at them to put on their shoes, and continued yelling at them to get out the door. I forgot to pack their lunches. We prayed for about two minutes. I screamed Bible verses at the backseat of my car. On the way to school I quizzed them on their spelling words, and we listened to '80s music. I told them it was Christian music. #yougottahavefaith.

After they got out of the car, I drank leftover Coke while eating the half-melted leftover M&M's I found in the bottom of my purse. I considered listening to the Bible on my phone, but I chose Dax Shepard's new podcast with Jimmy Kimmel instead. I drove past the gym in favor of going to TJ Maxx. I walked aimlessly up and down the aisles, and I bought two throw pillows, some pesto spaghetti sauce, gummy bears, and a Coca-Cola in the checkout aisle. #breakfastofchampions

I went home and checked Facebook to see if people liked last night's post about my new haircut, and I scrolled through friends' European vacation photos and adorable family videos for about 30 minutes. Then I checked Instagram and Twitter to see who liked me today. I thought about doing my devotions, but the phone rang and I forgot. I cleaned my kitchen floor from cereal crumbs and spilled milk. When I looked up, it was noon and I hadn't had a shower! #MondayMorningCrushingIt

Unfortunately, I can't blame my kids for my crazy. I wasn't any more put together before they came along. I just thought the older I got, the more peaceful and content I would become. When I started doing stand-up comedy, I had a feeling way down deep in my gut that I was finally in my lane. I had found something I was good at and a place where I could be used by God. I began doing clubs, and I was very open about my Christian faith on stage. As long as it was funny, audiences were cool with it.

Then people began coming up to me in the clubs after shows and asking if it was all an act. When I said no, sometimes they would ask me to pray for their sick grandmother or something like that. I realized that doing stand-up comedy was my ministry, and even though it didn't look like what others were doing, I was right where God wanted me to be. It was as if God was saying, "Go out there and show the world I can use anyone. Even you!"

I was having the time of my life, and the next thing I knew, I was asked to do comedy in a church. I didn't know that was allowed. Did Christians laugh in church? Turns out there was a whole world of Christians doing comedy, and I've had the opportunity to tour with everyone from Tim Hawkins to Bob Smiley to Sherri Shephard (from *The View*), and many more. I found out I wasn't the only Christian who was funny. I did music festivals and cruises, and I hosted part of the Gospel Music Awards at the Grand Ole Opry. My career was taking off like a rocket, and it was all because I had said yes to the plan

God had for me: to do stand-up comedy instead of trying to just be an actress on film and TV.

I still kept one foot firmly planted in Hollywood, but I was touring the country, doing stand-up about 40 weekends a year. It didn't slow down when I got married, or when I had two kids. We just loaded them up and took them with us. I became a spokesperson for Christianity in Hollywood, and I was proud to do it. Yes, it was crazy and unpredictable, but it was new and exciting and I loved every minute of it. It's pretty amazing to be smack in the middle of God's will for your life. You can try to make things happen on your own, but when God is with you, you experience a certain type of favor that is nothing less than supernatural. It's not easy by any means, but it's sort of an indescribable knowing you are right where God wants you to be.

You can try to make things happen on your own, but when God is with you, you experience a certain type of favor that is nothing less than supernatural.

And charting unknown territory is fun. If I'd been warned about all the pitfalls and potholes on this crazy journey, I can guarantee you'd be getting your coffee from a very funny barista named Kerri. I'd be working at Starbucks and getting benefits.

When you work in entertainment, your career doesn't head in a straight line upward year after year. Most people in the entertainment industry have a career path that looks the stock market if you jotted it in terms of success. And really, how am I defining success anyway? I'm a single mom supporting two kids, and I love what I do. But it takes hustle every day to stay relevant in my marketplace and gainfully employed. This job is not for the faint of heart. And this past year of my career has been one of the more difficult ones I can remember.

My mother freaks out every time I almost get a big job. Most of the time the promises get broken. I've learned to translate the words, "Yes, we're definitely doing this" to actually mean, "Maybe we'll do that thing we talked about, but don't call us. We'll call you." I've come to accept there are ebbs and flows, but 12 years in, it's not becoming easier. In some ways it's harder. I have two mouths to feed and a mortgage, so there's more on the line.

This past month has been somewhat of a blur. One night I was at a totally amazing prayer meeting. We were praying for God to move and heal people, and I felt awesome. Then I came outside to find that my car fender was literally lying in the street. Most of my parked car had been totaled. All I could think was, *God, that girl we prayed for to get healed of her fibromyalgia had better get well if this kind of warfare is going on!* Turns out, a drunk driver hit my car, along with four others. My damages were in the ballpark of $5,500.

Around that time I also had to have some minor outpatient surgery on my sinuses. (After the age of 35 you have to start having minor procedures to fix things. You become more like a car.) I had complications with the anesthesia, so the recovery was three times longer than predicted, and I was in lots of pain. Nonetheless, I had to get on a plane and perform in Arizona for an event I was headlining at a church. I never mentioned to them I was recovering from surgery because I didn't want them to be worried I wouldn't come. I don't miss shows— no matter what. I had my prayer warriors praying for me, and with adrenaline and Jesus, I managed to pack for my trip.

The morning of the show I got a call from the drunk driver's insurance company. They were refuting the charges against the driver. (Even though he got a DUI and went to jail.) They would not be paying for any of my damages until further notice, maybe 30 to 60 days. My insurance said I didn't have collision coverage, so they couldn't pay me one dime either.

(Note to everyone reading this: Get collision coverage on your car.)

I was so upset I almost cried, and the insurance lady was so mean to me. I think she has a bright future as a dictator. I hope they recorded our call for quality assurance. I called my mom, and she was comforting when she said, "Well, God has a plan, and maybe you'll sell lots of books tonight to help pay for your car." I appreciated the thought, but she was oversimplifying matters. That's okay though, since she's my mom.

I got to the airport hyped up on Claritin-D, nose spray, and Excedrin Migraine. I made it to the plane in mediocre pain, only to hear the captain say we'd be delayed on the runway for some time. I was going to have to rush to my gig. When we landed in Phoenix we had another delay on their runway. Thank you, Southwest. I love you guys, but I could go for fewer jokes and more flying.

I was picked up at the airport, and I made nice small talk with my driver as I gulped down a Coke and some nuts, trying to get some energy. My shows really start from the moment I'm picked up. Everyone expects me to be funny at all times, even if it's five o'clock in the morning. But I don't mind; I like meeting people.

I arrived at the event, where I was scheduled to do two shows, and I was told they were both almost sold out. Around 1,000 women were coming to see me, and they had planned for 350, so they had to move venues. Now, for every three shows I have like this, I have one where I'm sitting in a church nursery praying to God we have enough people show up to fill the front rows so I don't feel like a total failure. But that night, even though I had a stomach infection and a splitting headache, I said a prayer of true gratefulness to God. I realized without Him none of this was possible. He's really my best agent and promoter.

I felt good about myself and the work I was about to do. I was doing comedy, but I was also doing some ministry, sharing a testimony, and probably making a salvation prayer. I try to make those invitations as much as I can at shows, if they let me. What's the worst that can happen? They fire me? I'm leaving the next day anyway, and I already have the check. But seriously, most churches let me do what the Holy Spirit leads me to do.

I realized without Him none of
this was possible. He's really
my best agent and promoter.

As I waited in the green room alone, the adrenaline was flowing, but I was still dealing with a bad headache. I texted several of my prayer warriors and asked them to pray for strength, energy, and pain relief. I snacked on salami and fruit, and then I hit the stage. In His true fashion, God did not let me down. It's sort of like an out-of-body experience when I am up there. I've literally been hoisted onto stages in all sorts of pain, and something magical happens and I'm able to perform.

The crowd was on fire. They laughed and cried. (It was better than *Cats*.) I had a ball. It felt so good to be doing what I love in front of an appreciative audience. They were all hyped up on coffee and desserts, which helped too.

I came back to my green room, and even my head felt much better. I had about 20 minutes to spare, so I texted my prayer folks to share the good news. Then I went to check my trusty Instagram account to see who thought my last post was "adorable #blessed." And that's when I saw it.

As I was scrolling through pics of kids and cats and vacations, I saw a friend of mine had booked a guest-starring role on a major TV show. Suddenly I was as green as the Incredible Hulk with envy. It only took three seconds to make the transformation. I could feel the blood rushing to my head, my heart pounding, and my soul crying out silently, "Why, God? Why am I not guest starring on Showtime?"

Mind you, this show is so dirty that when I tried watching it once I had to turn it off because it was so offensive. But it certainly would have been nice to be asked to be on it! And then, to put the stake in my heart even further, I scrolled down to see another friend of mine had sold her film to a network, and she was on set, shooting. I had had meetings with the same network, pitching my two films. They had said, "We love this. We're definitely doing this!" And we remember what that means, right? That was five months ago.

Gone were all the feelings of job satisfaction. I couldn't even enjoy my complimentary olives and meats in the green room. I couldn't bask in the joy of stealing the granola bars for my kids' lunch. (Half of what my kids eat in their lunches has been confiscated from my green rooms, Delta Crown room lounges, or hotel lobbies. Don't judge me! You know you do it too…or you should!)

Anyway, I had this dark reaction to seeing my friends' success, and I didn't like it. So I took Instagram off my phone…*again*. Deep down I was happy for my friends. I mean, I love them. They both worked hard. But so did I. And here I was pleading with strangers to buy my books so I could buy a new fender for my 2009 Ford Taurus and bootlegging snacks in my purse to feed my children. Was this what the glam life was supposed to look like? People think I'm rich and sorta kinda famous when they see me on stage or in social media. Don't they know I shop at the Dollar Tree, and for more than paper towels?

I had to pull it together and get back out there on that stage. I said a silent prayer: "Dear Lord, I'm grateful for this opportunity to go do this. Sorry for being an idiot."

The second show went better than the first. I did my comedy and shared personal stories about what God has done in my life. I felt led to share my daughter Ruby's healing story, from being sick in the NICU to being a bouncing, pouncing, award-winning seven-year-old. Women gave their lives to the Lord during my show, and I was on such a high. When I came out afterward, I saw the lines were enormous, with more than enough people waiting to buy every book, CD, and DVD I had. But more importantly, women were coming up to me as they often do to talk and pray with me.

First, there was a woman who heard Ruby's story and tearfully told me she just got out of the hospital herself and was caring for her daughter. She also had a daughter who was born with challenges; she was nonverbal and would face medical hurdles her whole life. As I hugged her and prayed with her I could feel God over our shoulders, smiling down on us. It was just the beginning.

Women were encouraged by my faith journey, and they were full of faith to believe for their own lives. I had the honor of praying with a girl who beat cancer at 13 years old, but now she was 16, and it had come back. She asked the Lord to help her have peace in the storm.

I met a mom of seven. She was dealing with severe depression and wore a diabetes pump. We prayed together, asking God to help her suffering. The list goes on and on. I don't know how long I stayed praying with women that night, but we closed the place down. I wasn't about to leave until every single person who wanted prayer got it. I didn't feel any headaches or stomach pains. I was smack-dab in the middle of where God wanted me to be, and I was high on life.

Time passed so quickly, and when it was over, I came back to my hotel room and felt like I could fly. I was starting to feel the physical exhaustion setting in and my body was aching a bit. But I felt humbled. I wouldn't have traded places with anyone for any job in the world. I had the privilege of being a part of these women's journeys, big and small. They told me they needed to laugh. They said they needed to be encouraged, and God gave me the ability to do that. God is such a show-off. I sat in my room adding up the money I'd made that night. It was much more than I expected, and it was a nice start to paying for my car.

I wondered if the Israelites felt that way when God gave them literal manna from heaven every single day. When they screwed up and doubted Him, when they were filled with discontentment and jealous for their old lives in Egypt, God didn't abandon them. When they came to their senses, God was there to feed and clothe them and supply exactly what they needed. God was never late, and God knew there was a promised land waiting for them if they would stay on the path He set out for them.

Here are a couple of the verses that have always spoken to me in tough times:

> Trust in the LORD with all your heart
> and lean not on your own understanding;
> in all your ways submit to him,
> and he will make your paths straight.
> Do not be wise in your own eyes;
> fear the LORD and shun evil (Proverbs 3:5-7).

I had had to trust in the Lord that night. I had to go to Arizona and do what He wanted me to do. If I hadn't been in Arizona that night, maybe there were women who wouldn't have been saved. The enormity of that is something I don't stop and ponder very often. Now, yes, I'm sure there are others He would have used if I had said no. But He allowed me to be part of the equation. He allowed me to experience the joy the disciples felt when they walked with Jesus, learning about sharing the gospel of His love and the hope we can have in Him.

I don't usually hear from people after my shows, but that night my inbox on social media was flooded with messages of thanks and even pictures taken. My favorite one was a black-and-white photo of four of us, huddled together praying and seeking the Lord. You can't put a price on that. I'm glad I stayed the course and showed up. I still think about those women I met, and I hope to hear more stories of what God did for them that night. But more that, I hope I get to meet those women in heaven. I want to see the women who said yes to being saved one night in Arizona when a comedian took the stage. I pray God continues to give me more opportunities to minister. (And I'm totally open if He wants me to do comedy and an altar call on HBO.)

So I know you may not be a comedian or someone who gets up in front of thousands of people on a regular basis, but did my story strike a chord with you? Have you struggled with jealousy in your job or maybe even with friends or family? Does it sometimes seem as if everyone else has it easier than you do? Do you feel as though you are always the last in line when it comes to getting what you want out of life?

I want to see the women who said yes to being saved one night in Arizona when a comedian took the stage.

I don't have the exact solution for us on this one. But I do know it helps me to take a step back and look at reality when the jealous chord strikes. The enemy is really great at twisting things up in our minds and evoking emotional knee-jerk reactions. These friends of mine who posted about their moments of success haven't had a free ticket to easy street. I know this for a fact. I also know they've both worked extremely hard in this thankless business, and for every yes there have been hundreds of nos. Neither of them can do what I do, and vice versa. In reality we're not in competition with each other; that's just what the devil wants me to think. Taking an honest look at our situations and eliminating the competitive thoughts can sometimes help diffuse the jealousy, which is not from God. It's just Satan trying to distract us from our own calling and path.

Take a moment right now to think about where God has you. Whom are you influencing? Is it your family? Your kids? Other coworkers? Friends? Your parents? Maybe you're the only Christian some people are ever going to meet. That's your ministry right there. Your job is not to run up to them with matches and say, "It's hot in hell!" Your job is to be you, and for you to be their friend the same way Jesus is. God has something specific and special for every one of us. Believe it.

God has something specific and
special for every one of us. Believe it.

Can you think of an area where God can use you? My mom and dad make beautiful handmade cards and send them to people who need a little lift. People are so blessed by the unexpected gesture, and that's my mom and dad's ministry. Maybe you make really good soup. Can you bless someone who might need a hot meal? Are you a really good listener? Make a phone call to a friend who needs someone to talk to. When we are busy serving others, there is less time to worry about competing with them. It helps you remember we're all in this together.

For those of you who are gifted in the art of cooking or baking, please email me for my personal address. I'm open to helping you use your gifts.

These verses are good to think about and commit to memory when you are struggling with feelings of jealousy:

> Now there are varieties of gifts, but the same
> Spirit; and there are varieties of services, but the
> same Lord; and there are varieties of activities,
> but it is the same God who activates all of them
> in everyone (1 Corinthians 12:4-6 NRSV).

> For we are God's handiwork, created in Christ
> Jesus to do good works, which God prepared
> in advance for us to do (Ephesians 2:10).

> Love is patient, love is kind. It does not envy, it does
> not boast, it is not proud (1 Corinthians 13:4).

And I saw that all toil and all achievement spring from
one person's envy of another. This too is meaningless,
a chasing after the wind (Ecclesiastes 4:4).

12

MY HEART IS BREAKING FOR HOLLYWOOD

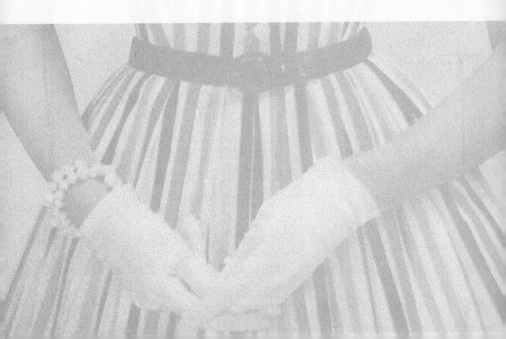

've been an out-of-the-closet Christian in Hollywood for many years now. (There are four of us.) I could say it's been an uphill battle and I've had to fight tooth and nail for any success I've had in this town, but that's not true. I can't say I've faced much opposition for being a person of faith at all, at least not to my face. I do think it's a battle to produce projects that are in any way family friendly or even faith-based. It's hard to earn any street cred from the powers that be here in Tinseltown.

I've always felt like a square peg in a round hole. I'm a Christian, but the Christian industry people mostly live outside of California. I often get pegged as "too edgy" because I chose to stay here, though I am definitely way more G-rated in my comedy than 90 percent of my fellow LA comics, actors, and director friends. I never found my place. So I've paved my own path, baby step by baby step, and I've just chosen to keep on walking.

I've always kept plugging away, knowing there is no job I'd rather have. I love to create, tell stories, and bring laughter to crowds who need a bit of joy in this often-dark world. And I honestly don't think much about what's going on around me in the entertainment industry most of the time. Of course, there are obvious moments I can't ignore, such as when the movie *Fifty Shades of Grey* came out. I was disgusted. I'm vocal about why this movie is a disgrace to women for so many reasons. Yes, I have plenty of my Christian friends buying these books and reading them at the beach in their brown paper bags, as a friend of mine confessed. These ladies also love the Disney Channel and attend church on Sundays. I've tried arguing with them, but I just ended up feeling as though I'll never get my point across to someone who doesn't want to hear a different perspective.

I never found my place. So I've paved my own path, baby step by baby step, and I've just chosen to keep on walking.

I remember 24 hours last spring that were particularly challenging. It started out one day when my writing partner pitched two of our family-friendly film projects to a TV executive team. The meeting went well, and they asked us to do rewrites from their notes as soon as possible. My partner and I burned the midnight oil and worked hard to turn in everything the next day. We are both moms, so multitasking is our specialty. The next day we were on the phone with our producers, and we were celebrating the positive feedback on our sweet, simple rom-coms. I can't tell you how much of dream it would be to write movies like this and get paid for it! I could pinch myself. Nothing has officially sold yet, but you must enjoy every step, or all the stress, pressure, and rejection will kill your soul.

So, after getting my kids from school and watching Lucy in her championship basketball game (for nine-year-olds), I met some friends for a movie night. My friend picked the movie, and we were all excited to see it. I knew it was rated R, but I'm a grown-up and I can handle a little blood and guts—which is what I thought the R rating was for. I hadn't read any reviews and just knew it was a spy movie. So we bootlegged popcorn in our purses, smuggled in water bottles, and settled in the theater for a great night of action and intrigue.

The start of the movie shows the actress as a prima ballerina and she's using a foreign accent, so I couldn't help but crack jokes. I am a comedian. It's in my genes. Then the movie took a dark turn I did not expect. This movie was not only sexually graphic and violent; it took things to a whole other level into what I would call "abusive porn."

The lead character is raped in the first five minutes, she kills two people in the throes of passion, and then she is trained as a spy, and to do that, she needs to use all her sexual prowess. Those training sessions were something I had never seen before. To say I was disturbed is an understatement. I was so emotional I left the movie 15 minutes in, all choked up in tears.

I ran to my car in the parking garage, and I sobbed, which was not like me. I'm not a huge crier, but my heart felt as though it had been broken into a million pieces. I was sad for actresses who have agents and managers telling them that in order to be the best they have to push the envelope and bare it all. Not only do they and the rest of their casts expose themselves, they glorify the abuse of power and sexuality for the sake of a plotline. Really? Whatever happened to spy movies like the ones with Chevy Chase and Dan Aykroyd (*Spies Like Us*) or Steve Carell (*Get Smart*)? Thinking this is where Hollywood is going crushes me for so many reasons.

It grieves me as a mom of a daughter who might want to pursue acting. How in the world could she expect to have any career? She's been acting since she was a toddler, and she's even been booked on a sitcom for NBC and a movie that went on to win an Academy Award. We turned them both down. We turned down Ron Howard and Spike Jonze and Joaquin Phoenix. The scripts were not clean, and I couldn't sell my child's soul for some college money…even a lot of college money!

I've turned down many roles in my career, and I don't ever look back with any regret. But in today's culture it's the norm to show this kind of perversity and call it art.

That day in my car I felt so alone. I didn't know what to do about a problem that seems to be infiltrating culture like a plague. I didn't know how I could do anything that would make one bit of difference. I reached into my purse and pulled out a Snickers for comfort. I wiped my nose and said to God between bites and snivels, "Oh God, I'm sorry for what we've done. I'm sorry for how we've perverted something You created to be beautiful into something offensive and demonic. I'm so sorry that discussing purity is now something to be compared with a history lesson, and *chastity* is a word almost never even mentioned. If You want me to write clean movies or create projects that inspire people, please open the right doors."

I didn't know what to do about a problem that seems to be infiltrating culture like a plague.

At times I've felt like my quest as a writer in Hollywood has been a little bit like swimming upstream in quicksand with shackles tied around my body. A war is going on out there against Christians, but it's mostly in the spirit realm. People don't come up to my face and say they don't like me. But I cannot tell you the number of times I've pitched a clean, faith-based project and it's come so close to getting made, but then something happens at the last minute to derail it. I had one project I was super excited about and the deal was ready to be signed, but then a family of reality stars decided they wanted to enter Christian entertainment, and there went all the budget. The producers holding the pocketbook were more than happy to take a chance on them because of their existing media fame.

I'm not trying to begrudge the success of others. I know we each have our own lane to stay in. I just wish mine wasn't so bumpy sometimes. God says He is looking for willing servants, and I'm here with several of my talented friends who are also Christians, but it's hard for us to catch a break.

The enemy wants us to back down while he continues to exploit artists in Hollywood, buying their souls with fortune and fame. As I sat there in my car that night, the thought occurred to me that pastors for ages have challenged us to pray, "Lord, break my heart for what breaks Yours." That's not an actual verse in the Bible, but it seems like a valid prayer. Was that what was happening to me? Maybe I should be thankful I'm not so lukewarm, like the churches John wrote to in Revelation 3:16.

Maybe I should be thankful I am in tune to recognize the things that break God's heart. Sin is painful to see when we're really looking through God's eyes. I think the devil has done a bang-up job for centuries desensitizing us, generation by generation, to things we should find offensive.

I was dumbfounded when a very respected pastor friend of mine openly admitted loving the HBO show *Game of Thrones*, even though it includes pornographic scenes that show full-frontal nudity and violence to women. Don't get me started on the list of other shows on the air that show nudity, violence, and graphic sex scenes that Christians left and right are streaming in the privacy of their homes without an ounce of remorse. I mean, this pastor (whom I truly love) had no issue with a show like *Game of Thrones*. So it made me wonder if I'm the one who was being prudish. I often feel like I am the last man standing, even in the Christian world. Am I the only one experiencing complete heartbreak over where Hollywood is taking us? But then again, am I part of the problem?

Here I was, freaking out and having a fit over this movie, yet I had just finished watching two seasons of *Crazy Ex-Girlfriend*, where everyone slept with everyone. I justified it as okay to watch because it was a musical comedy. My daughter and I just watched the old musical *Guys and Dolls*. Midway through the movie, Lucy said, "So, Mom, those guys made a bet they could get that Christian lady Sarah to go out of the country and get her drunk?"

I nodded quietly and said, "Um…uh…yes, dear. Now, never mind that. The gamblers are dancing!"

Look, guys, I won't let my kids watch Disney Channel because the kids have attitudes, but my girls have seen every single season of *Golden Girls* and the first four of *Gilmore Girls* until Rory went to college and started making bad choices. (Yes, kids, Logan is bad news. And don't drink the punch at college parties.)

I've come to the conclusion that I cannot control the likes and dislikes of others. I cannot get out a picket sign every time an A-list actress takes off her clothes. I'd be so tired.

I was being affected by that movie in an intense way because I am not closed off to the Holy Spirit convicting me of sin. And that is a good thing. God enlightened me to feel compassion for all those people who are seemingly enjoying worldly success while they compromise their values and convictions. The devil is keeping them just successful enough to feel they don't need God. And it might cost them their soul. The old saying goes, "Don't make a deal with the devil." I believe the devil is making deals every single day, and he's a lot more subtle than people realize.

"A little compromise here and there won't hurt," he says. "God isn't really that concerned with the tiny details. He just cares about the bigger picture and whether you're a good person or not. You don't actually have to change your lifestyle to get into heaven." He deceives us all the time. If you want to read more about this, check out C.S. Lewis's book *The Screwtape Letters*. It's a timeless classic on the art of persuasion from the perspective of a demon in training.

I read in the Bible about what happens when we become immune to the Holy Spirit, and it's not pretty. I do not want to be in that position.

> **God enlightened me to feel
> compassion for all those people
> who are seemingly enjoying worldly
> success while they compromise
> their values and convictions.**

Here are some verses that can remind you about taking a hard stand against sin and why God will honor you for it.

> I know your deeds, that you are neither cold nor hot.
> I wish you were either one or the other! So, because
> you are lukewarm—neither hot nor cold—I am about
> to spit you out of my mouth (Revelation 3:15-16).

> Do not love the world or anything in the world. If
> anyone loves the world, love for the Father is not in
> them. For everything in the world—the lust of the flesh,
> the lust of the eyes, and the pride of life—comes not
> from the Father but from the world (1 John 2:15-16).

> You are the salt of the earth, but if salt has lost its
> taste, how can its saltiness be restored? It is no
> longer good for anything, but is thrown out and
> trampled under foot (Matthew 5:13 NRSV).

I'm thankful my heart breaks for what breaks God's. I'm thankful my heavenly Father loves me so much that He doesn't allow me to become jaded and immune to situations where He wants to use me. I know God has given me gifts and talents. I'm not packing my bags and giving up. I'm going to stay in this crazy town, and I will continue to write stories and create projects God can be proud of.

I heard a pastor put it ever so bluntly: "Don't go see movies that would make God puke!" (That's what happens when you let the youth pastor preach on Sunday morning. But I never forgot his message. He's now a head pastor and a great one at that!)

What can you take from all this, my fair reader? Well, I'm glad you asked. We Christians are known for our angry boycotts that don't usually accomplish what we intended. Why don't we take a different route? Grab a camera. As they say, "YouTube is your oyster!" If you are an aspiring filmmaker, start right now. Make something fun and clean, and don't be afraid to follow your dreams. We need Christians in this business.

Are you a bit camera shy? Exploit your adorable children or your cats. People love cats, and I've never seen an R-rated cat video. Stop reading right now if you have, and give your life to Jesus!

But seriously, Hollywood is prowling around for the next YouTube sensation. Why not create something family friendly? (Hey, make some slime videos! Apparently those are killing it right now.)

Instead of focusing your energy on boycotts and negative talk, if you see a program on TV or film that supports your values, the best way to champion it is to buy a ticket or promote it to your friends. Use social media for something positive. Every movie and show has a hashtag on Twitter, and believe me, those producers are reading every single comment. If you do Facebook, find your favorite show's page and let them know you're watching. Views = Money! Hollywood speaks one language, and that is the language of the almighty dollar.

Also I've found out that our British friends know how to make great TV. Their shows are interesting and for the most part PG. We love BBC. We don't have to watch filthy content. We have choices. Every time you stream an R-rated program you are putting dollars in the producers' pockets. You're telling them to make more shows just like that. The same goes for when you stream something that is positive and uplifting. You can encourage those with money and power to make shows like that. Money talks, people! If we support them and buy the DVDs, we are sending a message that says we want to see more.

Sony Pictures and some of the other big studios have entire divisions now that cater to the faith-based audience. My dream is that faith and family programming someday will not look like a specialty niche market, but rather will be an integrated part of the lineup of shows and films made. We have a long way to go. But I'm not quitting. Are you? Please pray for me and the other Christians out here in Hollywood. We need your prayers.

And speaking of prayers, how about praying for specific people in the entertainment industry? Friends of mine started an organization called the Hollywood Prayer Network. They pray for specific people high up on the Hollywood food chain. I bet it's those prayers that have kept those folks from getting eaten by piranhas. Prayer changes things! And it could be the Holy Spirit giving you the nudge to intercede for someone you may never meet this side of heaven. Maybe your prayers will contribute to the battle for that person's salvation.

When A-list movie stars meet Jesus at the pearly gates, their résumés and great contributions to the betterment of society are not going to matter one bit. Top directors, actors, and celebrities will not be able to say, "Let me in! Don't you know who I am?" And sadly, very sadly, Jesus will say with His nail-pierced hands, "I never knew you. Get away from me, you who break God's laws" (Matthew 7:23 NLT).

Take a moment to let that sink in. The walk of fame will be for the ones who knew the real star…Jesus Christ! The Alpha and Omega. The beginning and the end, the God of heaven and earth.

When He comes back to judge the living and the dead, are you prepared to show Him your Netflix viewing history? If you're not, don't say I didn't warn you.

Now, if you will excuse me, I have some episodes of VeggieTales to stream!

TOP 10 THINGS I WISH I COULD
SAY TO MY YOUNGER SELF

1. You know how you can eat banana splits and pancakes for dinner, never gain an ounce, and people tell you that it won't last forever? You should keep eating all that stuff and enjoy every minute of it. Because they are not lying. And you are not the exception to the rule.

2. Your mom was right about some things, like dressing up to travel. It is never a bad idea, because you never know who you are going to run into or meet. Trust me!

3. Always carry wet wipes, a bleach pen, mints, lipstick, tape, and hair bands in your purse. You will be able to get out of any bad situation like Charlie's Angels did.

4. Never cut your own bangs or color your own hair. Certain things are best left to a professional. Don't scrimp on self-care. Oh, and use self-tanner with caution.

5. When you give birth, *get the epidural*! You do not get a prize for natural childbirth, and in this case, drugs are your friend.

6. There are some people in your life who will leave, though you think they will be there forever. It's okay, because new people will come into your life unexpectedly and you needed to make room for them.

7. Learn how to say no! This will serve you well later in life when you are asked to be on certain committees or groups you have no business joining. You were not called to be a youth leader, or a camp counselor in the woods, or sew costumes of any kind.

8. Life is going to throw you major curveballs, and you will be knocked down for a bit. You will get up. You will be okay. God was not caught off guard. Go to Him and His

Word. He will see you through. Memorize a few verses you can recite when you need them, like Isaiah 43:2: "When you walk through the fire, you will not be burned."

9. There is no significant proof that Coca-Cola can kill you, but running almost certainly will. (Sweating is overrated. Try Pilates.)

10. If you can avoid this thing called social media altogether, do it!

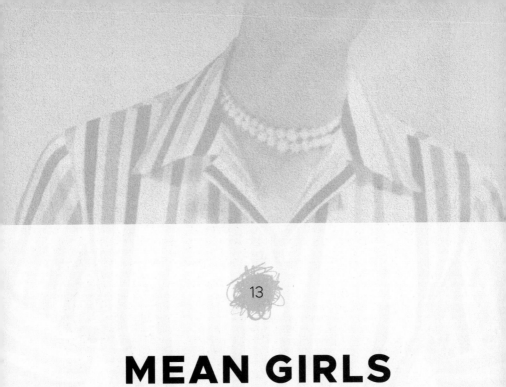

MEAN GIRLS

've never considered myself a mean girl, and I have my third-grade teacher, Becky Veenstra, to thank for that. In grade school I did have my moments, like the time I got in a fight with Kimmy Grandon in the girls' bathroom. I called her the unthinkable...*flat*! But a defining moment occurred in third grade when some of the kids were making fun of a girl on the playground and I didn't try to stop it. Mrs. Veenstra pulled me aside and changed my life with the words: "Kerri, I didn't expect that kind of behavior from you." That was all it took. I was in tears, and I set out to never be mean to any other kids on the playground ever again.

I went out of my way, and still do to this day, to make new kids feel included in every situation. Now, I will admit to being responsible for sharing some hilarious/gossipy stories behind people's backs. But as my mother always said, "It's not gossip if it's true!" The Lord did convict me of that later in life. Now I just tell gossipy stories on stage for a living, but I don't use names.

I know what it's like to feel rejected. The mean girls in eighth grade told me, and I quote, "There is no room for you at our lunch table." Yes, that really happened. I did what any other self-respecting girl would do.

I ran to the bathroom and cried, and then I told my mother I wanted to transfer schools. She didn't listen, and I eventually became friends with some of those girls. I later realized they came from some pretty tough home life situations and they were just acting out. The old saying is true: "Hurting people hurt people."

But I thank God for my friends Tracy Jambor, Susie Koster, Gretchen Cambra, and Cindi Toldstead. They didn't care about the mean girls in the lunch room, and they made room for me at their tables. I will never forget them and their kind gestures, and I don't know if they will ever realize how much their kindness meant to a mixed-up 14-year-old just trying to fit in. Note to parents: Please try not to move when your kids are in eighth grade. That's just torture.

As I've mentioned, I was a musical theater major in college, and I needed to escape the show tunes and parties where everyone got extremely experimental after 11:00 p.m. so I joined a sorority at the University of Michigan. I was really happy with my choice, and cramming 65 girls in one house seemed like a really great idea. We had bunk beds and tiny closets and phones with cords, so if you wanted any privacy you had to drag the phone out in the hallway, cord and all. We had theme parties and date nights and candlelight vigils. My dance ministry was solid at the Beta fraternity house, and it was a nice departure from other distractions like classes and learning.

I made some amazing friends, and I wouldn't trade any of it for the world. I wasn't exactly following Jesus wholeheartedly, but I did attend Bible study at my sorority house because there were free snacks. Robin brought them, and she made a difference in my life, though you wouldn't have known it then. I had the opportunity to perform for her organization, Campus Crusade for Christ, years later and I told her how much her coming to my Alpha Phi house every Wednesday with chips had impacted me and my destiny.

I made some incredible friends in that crowded brick house. One of my friends, whom we'll call Jackie, was a total soulmate of sorts. (For the rest of this chapter the names have been changed to, um…protect the guilty!) We roomed together and lived through all our boy dramas and traumas together. We had a lot of common interests, and we were certain we would be sisters for life. Nobody could make me laugh like Jackie. Even years later we could get on the phone and relive a bad date party story and crack up in tears.

I had a group of childhood friends I loved. I thought these women would be in my life forever.

That group of us stayed really close after high school and college. There were weddings, bachelorette parties, trips to Vegas, and celebrations of one another's life milestones. We were there through the first divorce and the first almost divorce and many other hard times. We celebrated the marriage of every one of us, although Jackie and I thought we were going to be the last spinsters on earth as we watched all our friends prance down the aisle and we caught their bouquets.

Now, it might seem like I'm describing the perfect Ya-Ya Sisterhood, where we shared every thought, hope, and dream with each other. But in reality, it wasn't like that. The friendships I made there were with girls I was thrown together with because of circumstances, not based on common likes or belief systems. No one talked about God or religion or political preferences or anything like that. The most controversial discussion occurred when we thought one of us might be struggling with an eating disorder because she was binging too much on ice cream.

One of the girls in my friend group—we'll call her Rachel—was my neighbor. She was lovable, but she was a little on the odd side. She craved a bit of controversy, and at times it got taxing. You know how you're studying political science and you're 20 and you know everything, and you have to convince everyone of this fact? She would say to me as I was walking out the door, "Why do you think communism is wrong? It isn't, ya know." I am never one to back down from a good discussion, but there was no winning with her. My friends and I just joked about it, and we loved her as she was. We all had our quirks. And besides, Rachel and I came from completely different backgrounds. If she saw me going to Bible study, I'm sure she thought I was an idiot.

As the years went by after college and lots of us moving away from home, it was harder and harder to gather everyone for reunions. Phone calls turned into group emails, and emails turned into social media chats. Our communication evolved with the times, and we all kept in touch as best as we could. We adored each other's cute kids on Facebook.

Looking back, I also realize that as we grew into adults and kept up with each other on social media, our personal beliefs and mindsets became more apparent. I was out in LA working three jobs and my friends were married to executives and starting supper clubs and taking vacations to Bora Bora.

Major political differences began to surface. I was a pro-life, card-carrying conservative, and all the others were pro-choice, liberal girls who thought I was completely small-minded. We never really fought about it seriously, just some good-natured ribbing when either of our candidates was elected. It was all in good fun. We did it all with humor.

Outside of our reunions, I didn't keep in phone contact with any of the girls other than Jackie. If I was in their city for a show, I'd visit. If there was an important milestone, I'd call. But those contacts became fewer and further in between. It wasn't on purpose, but we didn't have much in common at all. I watched most of my girlfriends evolve into women who traveled the world, threw extremely posh affairs, and lived a life I could appreciate but that did not share any resemblance to mine.

Rachel took great pride in telling us all about her beach house they were renovating on St. Martin's Island, even though Jackie was living paycheck to paycheck, and I was a struggling actress/comedian shopping at the Dollar Tree for milk. I didn't mind so much that we all were not as close. I had fun at the reunions, reliving and rehashing old memories and talking about various characters, but that's about as far as the connection went. But over the years the reunions felt more convicting to me and the less I wanted to attend. It wasn't as appealing anymore to sit around and "gossip" about the "good old days." God was doing something in me, and I was changing .

I had, however, made it a point to stay in contact with my girl Jackie. Outside of the crew, we had our own personal adventures. We went to Detroit, New York City, LA, and other places. It was our priority to do one getaway per year. During the year we didn't talk much on the phone, but we did make a pact one year to text each other our weight so we could see how much progress we were making before our summer beach trips. We never made much headway, so instead we'd text each other pictures of doughnuts. We decided to wear bathing suits with skirts and keep eating. So yes, you can tell our bond ran deep.

I didn't stop to think much about our relationship. But come to think of it, when I told her I was going through my divorce, all she said was, "Well, you've been strong with breakups. You will be fine." That was it. There weren't a lot of phone calls from Jackie, but thankfully I had plenty of good support here. Except for my one friend…we'll call her Claire, because that's her real name. She just wanted me to go work out with her, and that's not friendship. My real friends brought me chocolate and Ryan Gosling movies so I could eat my emotions. Okay, I'm kidding because even though Claire is my skinniest elliptical climbing friend, in times when I've needed her she's been there for me through thick and thin. If I could only get her to eat carbs with me, it would be the perfect relationship!

A few years ago, when Jackie and I were on one of our adventures in the Napa Valley, I asked if she had heard about any upcoming reunions because I hadn't. She said she hadn't either. But we had a great time together enjoying the countryside.

We parted ways and went back to texting pictures of brunch. It was our love language. About a month later I was having a truly glorious Sunday. You know those days that are so perfect you don't even have to record them on Instagram? I went to church with my family. I went to a park with my kids and actually played with them. I was so in the moment; I was very impressed with myself and my awesome parenting skills. The sun was shining, and all was right with the world.

As we pulled in our driveway, I grabbed my cell phone because, well, it had been several hours since I'd checked social media, and I'm sure I was starting to have tremors. I logged on to my ever-trusty Facebook, and there it was. I looked at my phone, blood rushed to my face, and I was filled with shock and awe. I couldn't speak.

The words that finally came out of my mouth sounded like,

"Ohhhhh, snap!" What I was "oh snapping" about were the pictures of *every single one* of my childhood friends in matching baseball caps in my hometown having a reunion at our favorite restaurant without my even knowing about it. I'm not kidding; it was *every single one* of them, Jackie included. It was like not getting invited to Chuck E. Cheese's when you were nine and then that kid bringing the pictures of the party to school on Monday morning!

There they were, arm in arm, without a care in the world. It was like a bad "Where's Waldo?" I mean, "Where's Kerri?" But Kerri was nowhere to be found. Kerri was *not invited*. Not only was Kerri not invited, but this was clearly a very thoroughly planned-out rendezvous that had been kept completely secret. That is until one friend did the unthinkable: she posted a million photos on Facebook.

Facebook *never* lies! There are no secrets on Facebook. Facebook is my friend. These women were not. But what was I supposed to do about it? This wasn't the third-grade playground where I could run and tell the teacher, "Um…all the kids went to Rocco's pizza without me and planned a weekend of fun activities and spa visits and I didn't even get a matching baseball hat!"

My eyes filled with tears, and my kids had no clue what was happening. We were parked in my driveway, and I couldn't even take them out of their car seats. I just sat there and tried to process my feelings through my snivels. I wasn't a grown woman at that moment, confident and living a fulfilled life. I was that third-grade girl who dreaded recess because of the deadly fear that no one would play with her on the playground. I was that fifth-grade girl who did a penny drop in the dead of winter off the monkey bars and broke her arm because she wanted to fit in with the sixth-graders. And because Kimmy double-dog dared me.

You see, as I said, I was never the girl who felt accepted, and I spent my life trying to fit myself into groups and friendship circles in an effort to feel a sense of belonging. Somewhere along the line, the enemy planted a lie in my head: "You are never going to be good enough for anyone to like you." I battled that lie all my life, and to be completely candid, it still pops up today. Just because we become grown-ups doesn't mean all our issues magically disappear.

Somewhere along the line, the enemy planted a lie in my head: "You are never going to be good enough for anyone to like you."

My kids tried to console me as I whined like a little girl, "I have no friends!"

Lucy said, "You have a million people who love you."

I replied, "No, that's not true. I have a couple of people on Facebook who like all my posts and have lots of cats. And I have that one stalker. I bet they think they are my friends!"

"But what about Gia and Cathy and all our church friends?"

"They don't count...they are family. They have to like me!" Lucy gave me a hug, and I sulked to my room and tried to come up with a plan. Now, mind you, I'm Italian, and sometimes that "Godfather/ Tony Soprano" mentality pops up. I have to remember that whole "turn the other cheek" thing wasn't in the Bible as a suggestion. I have some uncles who could take care of any of my problems with one phone call. (Just kidding...or am I?)

My gut reaction was to make a snarky comment on the pictures and then do that Mafia thing and unfriend all of them. That is the modern-day equivalent of "You're dead to me!" But I compromised and posted a comment: "Looks like fun!" I guess I wanted them to know I knew. Was this passive aggressive? Of course it was! Did I do it anyway? Of course I did! I'm no saint, and I felt like this was showing restraint!

I didn't know who to be mad at or what to say, but I felt the immediate urge to call Jackie. Her betrayal stung the most. I kept thinking of some logical explanation as to why she didn't tell me about the trip, or why she even went? So I called Jackie and tried not to sound too hysterical. I was mostly in shock, waiting for her to explain and then profusely beg for my forgiveness. Guess what? It never happened. I mean, not even close. Jackie was surprised I'd found out about it, and she couldn't really form complete sentences. All she did was keep babbling, "Um, well…I made a choice…I, um…didn't want to hurt you…I, um…thought it was best you didn't know…I'm, um…just… well…" It was nonsense.

I literally stopped her and said these words very, *very* clearly. "Jackie, I see that you made a choice. I see that you hid that choice from me, but can't you at least just say you are sorry?"

Even after that I didn't get a clear apology. She wasn't being mean. She wasn't trying to hurt me. And she wasn't overly emotional. And at that moment I realized she didn't have the skills to relate to me on a deeper level. Over the years she had stopped calling me on the phone and she'd told me she didn't have a lot of time for friends. I was expecting something from Jackie she could not give. I still loved her like a sister despite all of this.

After I hung up with her, I had a decision to make about whether I was going to forgive her or not. We are called to forgive people even when they don't tell us they are sorry. Who would it be hurting if I held on to unforgiveness? Just me. I was still so mad, though. And I wanted to react the way everyone else does when they get mad or hurt. I thought about posting something passive-aggressive on Facebook, such as, "Well, the devil is at work today, but I am stronger!" Then tag all of them.

I realized I didn't have the luxury, as a grown woman in Christian leadership, to express my woes on social media so I could receive the sympathy from people all over the world who supposedly care deeply for me, although we've never met. That would definitely be a route to take, but I couldn't.

Another lesson I was learning in that moment was that Christians should react differently to hurt than those who are not believers. Well, it's supposed to look different, anyway. I ran the emotional gamut between rage and self-pity. I'd learned that one of the women, Rachel, had intentionally excluded me when she planned this reunion. And then it made sense because I represented everything she hated. She didn't like religion or any conservative values. And the fact that I had made changes to my life as an outspoken Christian offended her. That's right, our faith is offensive, whether we know it or not.

I couldn't think of any other reason. We had never had a fight of any kind. And as I sat there in my fluffy chair, I heard the voice of God telling me to pray for Rachel and her family. To pray that they would get to know Him. To pray that they would know His Son. I didn't know specifically about her personal beliefs at that particular time, but if God was telling me to pray, then I needed to obey.

It was clear in my head that God was talking to me because there was no way I could have come up with that idea. So of course I cried even harder because of the sobering reality that the God of heaven and earth was speaking to me and asking me to be an intercessor.

I obeyed God and prayed for Rachel and her family to know Jesus. With God's help I prayed to forgive her. And I felt this release come over me. I had released her into God's hands. I forgave her, and I felt peace. It wasn't up to me to convict her of what she did. I might never talk to her again, but I knew I'd done the right thing, and God would bless me for it.

But how was I supposed to react to the other seven Benedict Arnolds? Did they even care about me? They had to have talked about keeping the secret from me, hadn't they? It's funny how I could have a spiritual communion moment with God one minute, then go right back into my flesh two seconds later. It was like I was having a physical reaction to this situation. I was either crying or my face was turning purple from my fuming rage. I needed to pray to God to get me off this roller coaster to nowhere good!

God didn't give me clear guidance on how to proceed after my prayer for Rachel, but I gave myself some time to think before doing anything else. This was a chance to minister to these girls and to be

God's witness, and that did not mean sending them Bible verses and telling them, "Repent or burn!"

That evening I sat down to my computer, and I emailed all the girls. I told them I was hurt about what had happened. I told them I was grateful because I was able to process my hurt and had some people pray for me, and the prayers made me feel a lot better. I told them I wasn't going to hold any grudges, and I didn't know what the future held for me and them, but I wished them all the best. I had no expectations on what I was going to hear back, or even if I would. But once again, taking the high road does come with a sense of peace. I had my closure. The rest was up to God.

The next morning I got a phone call from Samantha. She was the one who had taken the pics and posted them. She was so apologetic, and she said after she got my email she couldn't sleep because she felt so bad. She said she had watched me and my family on Facebook, and she was truly inspired to pray more because of me. She thought I'd never want to speak to her again.

But I said, "Sam, you know what you were feeling last night? That was God convicting your heart. I so appreciate your apology, and because I am a Christian I can forgive and forget. We don't ever have to speak about this again."

She was so relieved.

I'd love to tell you I got several more phone calls with heartfelt apologies, but I'd be lying. I didn't get any more calls. And you know what? It's all good. Now at least I don't have to get those emails from my friend trying to sell me her Mary Kay cosmetics. And I'm spared a lot of political emails and vacation photos from Brazil and Bali! If I want to see that kind of picture I can always look at the Kardashians' Instagram.

In the months that followed I had some time to reflect on my "friendships" within that group. And the following Bible verses came to my mind.

There is a time for everything,
and a season for every activity under the heavens:

a time to be born and a time to die,
a time to plant and a time to uproot,
a time to kill and a time to heal,
a time to tear down and a time to build,
a time to weep and a time to laugh,
a time to mourn and a time to dance,
a time to scatter stones and a time to gather them,
a time to embrace and a time to refrain from embracing,
a time to search and a time to give up,
a time to keep and a time to throw away,
a time to tear and a time to mend,
a time to be silent and a time to speak,
a time to love and a time to hate,
a time for war and a time for peace (Ecclesiastes 3:1-8).

Maybe my season with this particular group was over. Maybe it was for the best. Maybe we were going in two different directions. After all, we didn't enjoy the same activities or lifestyles or much else anymore. I had changed, and I'm sure they had too. Letting go is never easy, but God did tell us in the Bible there is a season for everything. And that's the one thing about seasons: they are always changing. We can try our best to hold on to the past and the people who came with it. But when God is moving us into a new season and a new place, He's doing it because He knows that is where we need to be for our growth and blessings.

**When God is moving us into a
new season and a new place,
He's doing it because He knows
that is where we need to be for
our growth and blessings.**

I'm sure you've gone through seasons in your life where there was an abrupt change, and you might have held on to the former things with all your might. But when you finally embraced the reality that God was behind that change, didn't you feel better? They say hindsight is 20/20, and although it was a painful experience, in some weird way I'm glad God moved me onward. I've kept in touch loosely with Jackie and some of the other girls, but it has never been the same. They had another reunion the next year and, surprise—I wasn't invited. And surprise—I found out on Facebook. I didn't make any Facebook photo comments or send any emails this time. You know what God told me to do? Pray. So I did and I had my answer on how to proceed. I had peace.

I sort of felt like Elsa in *Frozen* with God singing to me in my head, "Let it gooooo, Kerri." I let it all go, because if I didn't I was going to continue to be hurt over and over again. Jackie had made her choice, and I couldn't change her mind and try to make her value me more. So I had to hold my head high and move on with my life and pour my energy into relationships that were positive and healthy. We never had any angry parting and have stayed in touch since then. No hard feelings once I was able to process it all.

So that's what I did, and I can tell you God has filled my life with some amazing relationships, some old and some new, that truly fulfill me in every area He wants for me. I have my "Brunch Buddies," Gina, my travel BFF, and many others who fill my life with joy. I have Bible study women and prayer warriors all over the world who pray with me, and I have high school friends whom I see and visit, and yes, there are even some college chicks I still keep in touch with. I have great neighbors who cut my hair and make farm-to-table food for me. I have girls to play Bunco with and talk about our kids for the past ten years. I'm not lacking in the friend department, and that is something to be thankful for.

Take a moment right now to think about who God has placed in your life that you are thankful for. Don't let the enemy lie to you and tell you that you are all alone. I don't believe that's true at all. Maybe there is someone in your life who would love to hear from you. What if you got "oldschool" and actually called them on the phone…and *spoke* to them? We need friends to do life with. Don't let the busyness of all that's swirling around you stop you from connecting once in a while with a girlfriend.

Have you gone through a similar painful experience with mean girls? Even if it was many years ago, the hurt could still seem quite fresh if you haven't dealt with it. Our memories are powerful things, and the enemy is all too happy to keep those wounds fresh. When I began writing this chapter, I wondered if it was going to be difficult and emotional reliving this experience and missing my friends, especially Jackie. But the good news is, I'm okay. I'm healed. I'm good. And that's what God wants for you too.

I'm grateful we are on this journey together. We all know God has forgiven us for some pretty gnarly things. God is doing a transforming work in our lives every single day. It's not by our might that we can forgive those who have hurt us. The Bible is filled with verses we can read and meditate on to help us out. After all, God said in 2 Corinthians 5:17, "Therefore, if anyone is in Christ, the new creation has come: The old has gone, the new is here!"

God is doing a transforming work in our lives every single day.

We are not who we were yesterday or who we will be tomorrow. If you've given God control over your life and accepted Jesus as your Savior, you are on the path to greatness, girl! Just you wait!

As I wrote this book, I thought about the Proverbs 31 Woman's life. The Bible doesn't say much about her relationships with women, except those who were her servants. Do you think the gals got a little catty at the watering hole sometimes? Did they gossip about each other's husbands chillin' at the city gates? I guess I'll never know until I get to heaven and I can ask these questions directly.

I know this was a lot to take in, and I've shared several things I have learned from this particular experience. When one of my daughters comes to me in tears because of their own "Mean Girl" experience, I can talk to her from a place of empathy and compassion and tell her that God always has an answer if we ask Him. Take a moment to pray right now and see what God might bring to light about your female relationships, old and new. Is there anyone you need to forgive? Anyone you need to ask for their forgiveness? Is there anyone you feel God is telling you to let go? I never said it would be easy.

I'd like to say a prayer for you.

> Dear God,
>
> I pray for the woman who is reading this right now. There is so much pain in her heart that she doesn't even know where to start. I pray that You, in Your supernatural love and gentleness, will guide her and help her find the closure she so desperately needs from any hurtful thing that has happened to her.
>
> Please, God, wipe away every tear and every hurtful deed that was done. Erase the words that were spoken. Oh Lord, please replace those with the truth about Your daughter, that she is strong and wonderful. Remind her that You've been with her every step of the way. Give her amazing friendships in her life that will encourage her and fill her heart and soul. Take away any feelings of unworthiness or loneliness because we know You are the mender of our broken hearts.
>
> In Jesus's name,
> Amen

Here are some particularly meaningful Bible verses that have helped me with forgiveness.

For if you forgive others their trespasses, your heavenly
Father will also forgive you, but if you do not forgive
others their trespasses, neither will your Father
forgive your trespasses (Matthew 6:14-15 ESV).

And whenever you stand praying, forgive, if
you have anything against anyone, so that
your Father also who is in heaven may forgive
you your trespasses (Mark 11:25 ESV).

Then Peter came up and said to him, "Lord, how
often will my brother sin against me, and I
forgive him? As many as seven times?" Jesus said
to him, "I do not say to you seven times, but
seventy-seven times" (Matthew 18:21-22 ESV).

[Bear] with one another and, if one has a
complaint against another, forgiving each
other; as the Lord has forgiven you, so you
also must forgive (Colossians 3:13 ESV).

Be kind to one another, tenderhearted,
forgiving one another, as God in Christ
forgave you (Ephesians 4:32 ESV).

Judge not, and you will not be judged; condemn
not, and you will not be condemned; forgive,
and you will be forgiven (Luke 6:37 ESV).

If we confess our sins, he is faithful and just
to forgive us our sins and to cleanse us from
all unrighteousness (1 John 1:9 ESV).

And Jesus said, "Father, forgive them, for they
know not what they do." And they cast lots
to divide his garments (Luke 23:34 esv).

Let all bitterness and wrath and anger and clamor and
slander be put away from you, along with all malice. Be
kind to one another, tenderhearted, forgiving one another,
as God in Christ forgave you (Ephesians 4:31-32 esv).

One last note on the positive side of this. If God is asking you to
let go of some old relationships, can you look around and see someone
new that God might be leading you to invest some time with? Is He
highlighting a new person at work? A new neighbor or person you've
wanted to get to know better but can never seem to find the time?

Maybe you're feeling awkward about starting a new relationship.
I know it's seems so old-fashioned to actually invite someone for coffee face-to-face. But, to quote one of my favorite movies and the great
Humphry Bogart in *Casablanca*, "This might be the beginning of a
beautiful friendship."

Kerri@proverbs32woman.com

My Dearest Kerri,

First of all, let me say, I was quite pleasantly surprised to hear
from you. And no, that is not my Twitter account, so feel free
to report it. But please keep this email address confidential.
You would not believe the spam we receive up here. If you're
wondering about heaven, yes, there is Wi-Fi. Hell has dial-up
that never connects.

Well, my dear, you certainly have a lot to say, and you aren't
afraid of expressing your feelings...*all* of them. I think that is
lovely and refreshing. I read every word you shared. I've been
taking it all in, as we have plenty of time up here since we are
not on your earthly clock.

My heart breaks for women in your generation. The world you live in is much more complex. You all seem to be so busy and distracted from the simple things our Lord created for you to enjoy during your short lifetimes. I do not hear much about women taking in a sunset, enjoying a simple walk, or basking in the glory of the magnificent world that is all around them. I hear of women scuffling around like ants with their faces down, hard at work, and hardly ever looking up. Even when they are driving! (That is a discussion for another time. Cars! Just amazing!)

I think you may be right. All that technology you speak of is ruining a lot of the human experience. We lived a much more scaled-down existence, and in a lot of ways I'm grateful for that. There weren't as many things vying for my attention, and I had less to distract me from spending time with my heavenly Father and my family. Yes, we had big battles of our own, but I would guess you would not like all the manual labor. And should I even mention the snakes and scorpions we had to deal with?

All that technology you speak of is ruining a lot of the human experience.

You are much too kind with your sentiments about me. In all honesty, we have a lot more in common than you would surmise. But I suppose Solomon only had room for one chapter about me. He picked all my finest qualities and left out many others. I had to laugh about your mentioning Bathsheba and how she and her husband, King David, met. You would like both of them, and let me say this with all candor: you remind me of King David. I mean it, truly. He was a very out-of-the-box son of Jesse, so much so that Jesse forgot to even mention his name to Samuel when he came visiting and looking to crown a new king. While Samuel was sizing up the other brothers in the house, David was out in the fields, talking to the animals and probably flirting with the neighbor girls. But what I adore most about him is the fact that he didn't shy away from the reality that he was always a little different.

David knew he didn't have to change for God to choose him as His son. He didn't have to be someone else in order for God to anoint him for greatness. God loves an unlikely hero. God chose to use David in the mightiest of ways because David walked with Him. He had a personal relationship with God, both in the good times and in his darkest hours. In the Bible we see David's relationship grow and deepen, and it was a beautiful thing to behold. He cried out to God with the utmost humility, but also in utmost despair and doubt. David had many flaws, but he wasn't afraid to admit his sins and all the ways they troubled him.

You are correct when you state that many Christians through the ages project some image of a flawless life, and they believe in a God who demands perfection—or at the very least demands that humans strive for perfection daily....or else! This is not the God David knew, and it is certainly not the God I serve. I bet a lot of that self-loathing started when the photograph was invented—and then that thing you call Photoshop. Now I'm hearing about this new thing called filtering. When will it end?

We struggled with our identities as women, and your generation certainly did not invent jealously. In fact, the Bible is filled with jealous women. It never ended well for them. Can we say *Jezebel*?

You are also correct about our wardrobe. It was never as uncomfortable and awkward as what seems to be in vogue for you today. I don't know how you do it. But then again, we didn't have it easy. Remember, we lived in the desert and no one had closed-toed shoes! And we didn't have pedicures either. I know. *Horrible.*

So while I do envy some of your creature comforts, such as indoor plumbing, I don't envy the pressures you're all putting on each other. So much warfare is going on in every woman's mind at all hours of the day and night. I wish I could send them each a telegram saying, "Don't believe the lies. They are from Satan. You are beautiful and delightful just the way you are. Don't let him steal your joy!" But since I can't do that, I'm glad you wrote this book.

I read your words about all of your worries, hopes, and fears, and I think those are exactly the type of thing God wants to hear from His children. Who better to cry your heart out to than the One who holds the answer to your woes?

Who better to cry your heart out to than the One who holds the answer to your woes?

Take, for example, just one of the instances when David was at the end of his rope when his own son was trying to take his life and he was forced to live in a cave. The stress had physically taken its toll on his body. He faced the rejection of all of his friends, and his enemies persecuted him. He was suffering with severe bodily pain, just like you have. He had much guilt from his own sins. He felt unworthy. But he never once turned his back on God. I love the stories about David because he was so imperfect and so sincere with his heavenly Father. There were moments in David's life when you think he would have been disqualified from ever being of any use to the Lord's kingdom.

But in His ever-loving mercy, God picked up His son, dusted him off, and called him "a man after my own heart." Isn't that beautiful and amazing? The Maker of heaven and earth used such intimate words to describe this lowly shepherd boy, adulterer, murderer, and liar. God didn't look upon all of David's sins. He looked upon David's heart and his repentance.

I adore Psalm 38. I've enclosed it for you below. Read it and see if you don't find some familiar themes with your struggles and King David's. You both definitely know how to cry out to God. And we know He listens.

> A Psalm of David, for remembrance.
>
> O LORD, do not rebuke me in Your anger
> or discipline me in Your wrath.
> For Your arrows have pierced me deeply,
> and Your hand has pressed down on me.
>
> There is no soundness in my body
> because of Your anger;
> there is no rest in my bones
> because of my sin.
> For my iniquities have overwhelmed me;
> they are a burden too heavy to bear.
> My wounds are foul and festering
> because of my sinful folly.
> I am bent and brought low;
> all day long I go about mourning.
> For my loins are full of burning pain,
> and no soundness remains in my body.
> I am numb and badly crushed;
> I groan in anguish of heart.

O Lord, my every desire is before You;
my groaning is not hidden from You.
My heart pounds, my strength fails,
and even the light of my eyes has faded.
My beloved and friends shun my disease,
and my kinsmen stand at a distance.
Those who seek my life lay snares;
those who wish me harm speak destruction,
plotting deceit all day long.

But like a deaf man, I do not hear,
and like a mute man, I do not open my mouth.
I am like a man who cannot hear,
whose mouth offers no reply.
I wait for You, O LORD;
You will answer, O Lord my God.
For I said, "Let them not gloat over me—
those who taunt me when my foot slips."

For I am ready to fall,
and my pain is ever with me.
Yes, I confess my iniquity;
I am troubled by my sin.
Many are my enemies without cause,
and many hate me without reason.
Those who repay my good with evil
attack me for pursuing the good.

Do not forsake me, O LORD;
be not far from me, O my God.
Come quickly to help me,
O Lord my Savior (BSB).

Isn't that a beautiful psalm?

And if you keep reading—as you kids say, spoiler alert—you will find out that God did deliver David from all of his foes and every evil. God lifted up David to be one of the most beloved rulers in history. And of course, when we get into the New Testament, there are dozens of examples of God expressing how much He loves to comfort His children. Take the book of Matthew, for example. Let's look at Jesus's words when He spoke to the crowds.

> Come to me, all you who are weary and burdened, and I will give you rest. Take my yoke upon you and learn from me, for I am gentle and humble in heart, and you will find rest for your souls. For my yoke is easy and my burden is light (Matthew 11:28-30).

It's quite incredible in heaven, meeting all the people who were in the Bible and actually walked with Jesus on earth. Oh, and I can't even begin to exclaim the magnificent moment when I first met our blessed Lord Jesus. Words cannot describe it. My heart leaps at the very thought of Him. There is so much I'd love to tell you about what it's like up here, but we'll save that for another time.

Now look who's the one who's doing all the talking? I'm just excited to share my thoughts with you.

I better be getting along. A jam session is about to begin, and I dare not tell you who's playing, for fear you might faint. But there is so much more for us to talk about, and we will. You know how to find me.

I'm so very glad to know you, Kerri. You are a gem...a fiery one, at that. Just like your Lucy and Ruby! Keep up the good fight, dear one.

Let me close by sharing a little song I'm quite fond of. Maybe you've heard of it. It's not from the Bible, but I think it sums up some of the feelings I have about you and me.

Thank You for Being a Friend
Author: Andrew Gold

Thank you for being a friend
Traveled down a road and back again

Your heart is true, you're a pal and a confidant...
And if you threw a party
Invited everyone you knew
Well, you would see the biggest gift would be from me
And the card attached would say
Thank you for being a friend...
And when we both get older
With walking canes and hair of gray
Have no fear even though it's hard to hear
I will stand here close and say
Thank you for being a friend (I wanna thank you)...
And when we die and float away
Into the night the Milky Way [not the candy bar]
You'll hear me call as we ascend
I'll say your name then once again
Thank you for being a friend!

Thank you for being a friend, Kerri!

Your friend,
Grace (That's actually my real name).

P.S. Patrick says, "Nobody puts Kerri in the corner." (He said you'd get that.)

P.P.S. I'm still looking for that Clark Gable fellow your mom mentioned.

Keep up the good fight, dear one.

Kerri Pomarolli has been seen on *The Tonight Show*, Comedy Central, ABC, Lifetime, Netflix, TBN, and many more. She tours the country with her clean comedy and has collaborated with many, including Jim Carrey and Carol Channing. She is a writer for The Hallmark Movie Channel. She is a popular red carpet host and inspirational speaker. Her passion is to spread the gospel through her stand-up comedy, books, writing, screenplays, and ministry events. Kerri has written several books, and she lives by the sea in California with her biggest sources of comedy material: Lucy and Ruby. You can find more info at www.kerripom.com and www.facebook.com/kerripomarolli. She spends an unhealthy amount of time on social media so be sure to drop her a line. www.instagram.com/kerripom